Top 25 locator map
(continues on inside
back cover)

←

CityPack
Las Vegas *Top 25*

**JACKIE STADDON AND
HILARY WESTON**

If you have any comments
or suggestions for this guide
you can contact the editor at
Citypack@theAA.com

AA Publishing
Find out more about AA Publishing and the wide
range of services the AA provides by visiting our
website at *www.theAA.com/bookshop*

About This Book

ORGANIZATION

This guide is divided into six chapters:

- Planning Ahead, Getting There
- Living Las Vegas—Las Vegas Now, Las Vegas Then, Time to Shop, Out and About, Walks, Las Vegas by Night
- Las Vegas' Top 25 Sights
- Las Vegas' Best—best of the rest
- Where To—detailed listings of restaurants, hotels, shops and nightlife
- Travel Facts—practical information

In addition, easy-to-read side panels provide extra facts and snippets, highlights of places to visit and invaluable practical advice.

The shades of the tabs on the page corners match the triangles aligned with the chapter names on the contents page opposite.

MAPS

The fold-out map in the wallet at the back of this book is a comprehensive street plan of Las Vegas. The first (or only) grid reference given for each attraction refers to this map. **The Top 25 locator map** found on the inside front and back covers of the book itself is for quick reference. It shows the Top 25 Sights, described on pages 26–50, which are clearly plotted by number (**1**–**25**, not page number) in a south-to-north arrangement (except the excursions). The second map reference given for the Top 25 Sights refers to this map.

Contents

Planning Ahead

WHEN TO GO

With so many of its attractions under cover and not dependent on weather conditions, there's no off-season to speak of in Las Vegas. Avoid high summer if you don't like excessively hot weather, unless you plan to stay indoors. Check to see if the city is staging a major convention before deciding when to go as the hotels will be in demand and their prices higher.

TIME

Vegas is on Pacific Standard Time (GMT −8), advanced one hour for daylight saving time between early April and early October.

AVERAGE DAILY MAXIMUM TEMPERATURES

JAN	FEB	MAR	APR	MAY	JUN	JUL	AUG	SEP	OCT	NOV	DEC
13°C	17°C	20°C	25°C	31°C	36°C	40°C	39°C	34°C	27°C	19°C	14°C
56°F	62°F	68°F	78°F	88°F	98°F	104°F	102°F	94°F	81°F	66°F	57°F

Summer (June to September) can be incredibly hot and oppressive, with daytime temperatures sometimes soaring as high as 49°C (120°F).

Spring and autumn are much more comfortable, with average temperatures usually reaching 21°C (70°F).

Winter (December to February) sees average temperatures above 10°C (50°F). There can be the odd chillier day when you will need a jacket, and sometimes it can drop below freezing at night.

WHAT'S ON

January *Laughlin Desert Challenge*: The world's top drivers compete in an off-road motor race over rough terrain.
Las Vegas International Marathon (late Jan).
March *NASCAR Winston Cup Race* (early Mar): A major event on the racing calendar held at the Las Vegas Motor Speedway.
March *St. Patrick's Day Parade* (Mar 17): A parade of floats downtown kicks off other entertainment; Celtic bands, storytellers and dancers.

April/May *World Series of Poker*: The best poker players in the world compete for supremacy at Harrah's Rio, with the final two days taking place at Binion's Hotel.
June *CineVegas International Film Festival* (early Jun): Film debuts from studios, with celebrities attending the huge parties.
September *International Mariachi Festival*: A popular Mexican festival hosted by the Mandalay Bay.
October *Invensys Classic*: A major five-day golf

tournament played on three of the city's best courses.
December *National Finals Rodeo* (early Dec): During the 10-day finals, cowboys compete and the rest of the city goes country-mad, dressing up, line-dancing and feasting on barbecues.
New Year's Eve Celebrations: A huge New Year's Eve party held at Fremont Street.
Billboard Music Awards: Music celebrities gather at the MGM Grand Garden Arena to honor the world's best music.

LAS VEGAS ONLINE
www.vegasfreedom.com
The official website of the Las Vegas Convention and Visitors Bureau offers well-presented information on everything you could possibly need to know when planning your trip to Las Vegas. It also has a hotel reservation service.

www.lasvegas.com
For articles on local news, listings, events and other sources of information, try this useful site run by the respected *Review-Journal*, Nevada's largest newspaper.

www.vegas.com
This informative site geared to visitors has honest reviews of restaurants, bars, shows and nightlife, plus it gives access to hotel booking.

www.lasvegasgolf.com
To help you plan a golfing holiday in Las Vegas, this site has detailed reviews on all the courses open in Vegas and other US cities. It has specials on golf packages.

www.vegasexperience.com
This lively site is dedicated to the Fremont Street Experience. See what's going on at any time of the year and look for places to stay and eat.

www.gayvegas.com
The most complete site for gay locals and visitors to Las Vegas. It keeps up with the very latest information on clubs, bars, restaurants and organizations, plus lots more.

www.nightonthetown.com
For one of the most comprehensive and easy-to-use guides to eating out in Las Vegas, check out this site. The restaurants are listed under cuisine type and location.

www.cheapovegas.com
Geared to the visitor who wants to do Vegas on a budget, this fun guide provides comprehensive reviews and unbiased opinions with a humorous slant.

PRIME TRAVEL SITES

www.CATRIDE.com
Official site for the Citizens Area Transit (CAT), the company responsible for the Las Vegas bus system. Operate the fun route planner to discover exactly how to get from A to B.

www.fodors.com
A complete travel-planning site where you can research prices and weather; book air tickets, cars and rooms; pose questions (and get answers) to fellow visitors; and find links to other sites.

CYBERCAFÉS

Most hotels in Las Vegas have business centers and offer internet access to their guests. www.netcafeguide.com and www.cybercafes.com are up-to-date search engines enabling you to locate internet cafés all over the world.

Cyber Stop Internet Café
✉ Hawaiian Marketplace, 3743 Las Vegas Boulevard South ☎ 702/736-4782; www.cyberstopinc.com
🕐 Daily 7–2.30
💻 30 mins $8, 1 hour $12

Getting There

ENTRY REQUIREMENTS

All visitors require a valid passport, and all except Canadians must have an onward ticket. Visas may not be needed by UK, Irish, Canadian, Australian, New Zealand or other EU nationals staying less than three months—check with the embassy in your home country before leaving. Health and accident insurance is required.

MONEY

The unit of currency is the dollar ($), divided into 100 cents. Bills (notes) are in denominations of $1, $5, $10, $20, $50 and $100. Coins are 1 cent (penny), 5 cents (nickel), 10 cents (dime), 25 cents (quarter) and 50 cents (half dollar).

$5

$10

$50

$100

ARRIVING

McCarran International Airport (LAS) is served by direct flights from cities right across North America, and there are intercontinental flights from London, Frankfurt and Tokyo. It is worth checking for special deals from airline and flight brokers, in newspapers and on the internet.

19km (12 miles) 13km (8 miles) 6km (4 miles)

FROM MCCARRAN INTERNATIONAL AIRPORT

The McCarran airport terminal (☎ 702/261-5211; www.mccarran.com) is 4 miles (6km) southeast of the Strip, at 5757 Wayne Newton Boulevard. Many different companies run airport shuttle buses every 10 or 15 minutes from just outside the baggage claim area. They all cost roughly the same (about $4.75 to the Strip and $6 to Downtown) and normally operate between 7am and 1am. Most stop at all the major hotels and motels. Less expensive are the CAT buses (about $2) that operate from outside the airport terminal: No. 108 will take you to the Stratosphere, from where you can transfer to the 301, which stops close to most hotels along the Strip; and No. 109 goes to the Downtown Transportation Center. Taxis are also easily available outside baggage claim, and cost $10–$15 to the Strip, or slightly more to Downtown hotels. Stretch limos line up outside the airport waiting to take you to your destination; if you are tempted, try to share as they can be costly ($40 per hour). For those wishing to rent a car, all major car rental companies are represented inside the airport's arrival hall.

ARRIVING BY BUS

Greyhound/Trailways (☎ 702/384-9561; www.greyhound.com) operates services to Las Vegas from most cities and towns in California and Nevada. Tickets can normally be purchased just prior to departure. This is a convenient and inexpensive way to travel, although probably not the most comfortable. All Greyhound buses arrive at Downtown's bus terminal at 200 South Main Street (☎ 800/231-2222).

ARRIVING BY CAR

Interstate 15 from Los Angeles to Vegas takes you through some of the most breathtaking scenery of the Mojave Desert. The journey takes 4–5 hours depending on road, weather and traffic conditions (delays are often caused by construction work). Carry plenty of water and a spare tire, and keep an eye on your fuel level.

ARRIVING BY RAIL

Amtrak (www.amtrak.com), the national train company, does not offer a direct service to Las Vegas, but you can connect to the city by bus from other rail destinations in California and Arizona. Amtrak has talked of restoring the line from Los Angeles to Las Vegas, but at the time of writing nothing had materialized. Contact Amtrak (☎ 800/231-2222) for the latest details.

GETTING AROUND

Most of what you will want to see and do in Las Vegas is found along Las Vegas Boulevard, which is well served by buses. The boulevard is divided into two parts: Downtown, between Charleston Boulevard and Washington Avenue; and the Strip, comprising several long blocks—Sahara, Spring Mountain, Flamingo, Tropicana and Russell. Hotels on the Strip (between Hacienda Avenue and the Sahara Hotel) are also served by red and green Las Vegas Strip Trolleys, and in 2004 the first leg of a new multimillion dollar monorail was launched (see box ► 12), providing a welcome addition to the options for getting up and down the Strip.

For further information about Las Vegas public transportation ► 91–92.

HANDY HINT

Even if you use the first-rate bus and tram services to get around Las Vegas, you are still likely to have to walk some distance to reach your destination. Wear comfortable shoes and use sunglasses to protect your eyes from the blazing desert sun.

VISITORS WITH DISABILITIES

If you are a wheelchair-user, on arrival at the airport you will find shuttle buses with wheelchair lifts to get you into the city. You will also find easy access to most restaurants, showrooms and lounges. All the hotel casinos have accessible slot machines, and many provide access to table games. Assisted listening devices are also widely available. If you plan to rent a car, you can request a free 90-day disabled parking permit, which can be used throughout Vegas; contact the City of Las Vegas Parking Permit Office (☎ 702/229-6431). For further information ► 91.

Las Vegas Convention and Visitors Authority ADA coordinator
☎ 702/892-7525;
fax 702/892-2933

Living
Las Vegas

Las Vegas Now

Banks of slot machines at the New York–New York casino

Las Vegas is the entertainment capital of the world, where sleep is a mere inconvenience interrupting a continuous stream of fun and hedonism, and where everything is bigger, louder, flashier and trashier. From the moment you touch down at the airport or cruise into town along Las Vegas Boulevard, it will dawn on you that this is like no other place on earth. The

LAS VEGAS FACTS

- The population of the city is around 535,000, a rise from 125,000 in 1970.
- In 1970, about 7 million tourists visited the city; today, some 37 million tourists visit annually.
- There are more than 15,000 miles (24,000km) of neon tubing in the Strip and Downtown Las Vegas.
- Vegas Vic, the enormous neon cowboy sign in Fremont Street, is the world's largest mechanical neon sign.
- The casinos make around $26.5 million every day.
- There are more than 175,000 slot machines to take your hard-earned cash.
- Nearly all the great modern golf course designers have completed a project in Las Vegas.
- Seventeen of the 20 biggest hotels in the world are in Las Vegas.
- In May 1905, blocks of Las Vegas land sold for $150. In the 21st century, land on the Strip has sold for more than $1.7 million an acre.

WILDLIFE

• For exotic animals you need look no farther than the themed hotels—there are sharks and crocs at Mandalay Bay, dolphins and white tigers at the Mirage, Chilean flamingos and African penguins at the Flamingo, and lions at MGM Grand's ranch. To get a glance of Nevada wildlife in its natural environment, head out of town to one of the national parks. Birds of prey include owls and hawks; even eagles may be spotted in the skies above the Grand Canyon. Reptiles, which should be treated with respect, include desert iguanas, horned lizards, rattlesnakes and sidewinders. The best time to catch sight of the biggest lizard, the Gila monster, is in May. You might also be lucky enough to get a glimpse of a mountain lion, and beware of the black bear, which is increasingly wandering into human habitats.

Above: *Chilean flamingos grace the wildlife habitat at the Flamingo resort*

sheer scale of everything is overwhelming, and the Strip in all its blazing glory is a thing of wonderment. But one thing this crazy city will never allow you to forget is that the driving force of Vegas is gambling—and that's what keeps the adrenaline pumping. Be prepared for the most peculiar idiosyncrasies: people falling asleep on the sidewalk after a hard night's work at the tables; slot machines greeting you at the airport and in the restrooms; or playing keno (similar to bingo) at the table while you wait to be served in a café.

Where else can you capture a skyscape that includes the Eiffel Tower, St. Mark's Campanile, an Egyptian pyramid and the Statue of Liberty on the same block? Vegas can offer all this rolled into one. Themed hotels are an attraction in themselves, capable of transporting you into a world of make-believe, with fire-spewing volcanoes, magical dancing fountains, stomach-churning roller coasters and the very best in entertainment.

Spawned from an earlier trading post along the old Spanish Trail, Las Vegas or "The Meadow," as

Left to right: *Entering New York–New York; the Fremont Street Experience sound and light show; poolside gambling at the Tropicana*

Mexican Antonio Armijo named it, became a popular stop for its freshwater spring. The prospect of gold added to the lure and later the building of the Hoover Dam secured the city's future. The liberal state laws of Nevada allowed the growth of the casinos, and soon the little campsite in the fearsome heat and inhospitable desert developed into a city. Evolving from the early saloons, the first casinos and hotels were built in the Downtown area in the early 1930s, followed by the expansion of the Strip in the 1940s. Through the days of the Mafia, the Rat Pack (see box ► 14) and sleazy, tacky "Sin City," to the mega-extravaganza you will find today, Las Vegas has never ceased to dazzle, amaze and thrill.

QUICKER BY RAIL

• The 4-mile (6.5km) rapid transit monorail system, connecting eight major resorts on the east side of Las Vegas Boulevard, finally materialized in 2004. After decades of failed plans, the monorail now makes it easier to get around, helping to ease traffic congestion and allowing passengers a respite from the heat. It takes about 15 minutes to travel from end to end, and there is room for more than 200 people. There are plans to extend the line to Downtown and the airport in the near future.

So what continues to bring some 37 million visitors here annually—gambling millions of dollars in the process—and keep the city the second most popular destination in the world after Disney in Orlando? Las Vegas is an ever-evolving metropolis with a restless spirit that's part of its electric appeal. Hotels are regularly being torn down to make way for brand-new innovative ideas, and entertainment programs constantly change. There are now some 125,000 hotel rooms in the city—the MGM Grand is the biggest hotel in the world, with 5,005 rooms. The city is also a popular residential area, with a roll call of celebrities making it their home. This continued growth brings with it environmental problems

---

CENTENARY YEAR

• May 15, 2005 was the 100th anniversary of the founding of Las Vegas. A host of celebrations took place throughout the year, from extravagant parties and historical revivals to air shows and special wedding ceremonies. This mega spectacular paid homage to the people, places and events that have shaped the city's history.

CELLULOID CITY

• Las Vegas has been a popular film location since the 1930s, and numbers some top international successes among its credits. It was a hangout for Elvis while he starred in *Viva Las Vegas* (1964); for Sean Connery when he played James Bond in *Diamonds are Forever* (1971); for Tom Cruise and Dustin Hoffman in *Rain Man* (1988); for Nicholas Cage in four films, including *Honeymoon in Vegas* (1992); and, in both 1960 and 2001, for a horde of famous actors who appeared in the *Ocean's Eleven* films.

Above: The *Bellagio's glass-roofed botanical garden*
Above middle: *Tying the knot at the Little White Chapel, popular with celebrities*

such as water shortages and light pollution, but this could well herald a new generation of ecofriendly, conservation-aware construction.

Not formerly renowned for good cuisine, Vegas now boasts some of the top restaurants in the world, many run by celebrity chefs. Shopping has also come into its own in the last decade, with most top designer names moving in. Although Vegas is primarily an adult playground, there has been a conscious effort to attract families. Many hotels, like Circus Circus and Excalibur, are child-friendly, and there are great theme parks and other attractions to keep kids amused for hours. Thousands of people are

RAT PACK MEETS VEGAS

• In the 1960s, Las Vegas was dominated by a group of major stars collectively known as the Rat Pack. Frank Sinatra first performed at the Copa Rooms in the Sands Hotel in Vegas in 1960, with the likes of John F. Kennedy in the audience. This was the beginning of the Rat Pack's involvement with the city. Along with Sinatra, Dean Martin, Sammy Davis Jr., Peter Lawford and Joey Bishop (all of whom were in town filming the original *Ocean's Eleven*) dominated the scene and drew the crowds in droves.

following in the footsteps of the rich and famous and tying the knot in Vegas. Couples, including movie stars Bruce Willis and Demi Moore, and, of course, the King himself and Priscilla Presley, have joined Mr. and Mrs. Average from countries as far apart as Britain and Japan, to get married in style in some of the 50 or so wedding chapels.

You might be forgiven for believing Las Vegas is not synonymous with culture. But beyond the neon there are some great museums and galleries showcasing anything from old masters and original Picassos to flamboyant pop art. Also blending perfectly with all the light entertainment is ballet and opera. It's hard to imagine that just a few miles away from the man-made wonders is a world of natural beauty. Dramatic canyons and dams, sparkling lakes and a varied wildlife are light years away from the razzmatazz. The terrain lends itself to some of the finest golf courses and, in fact, Nevada is rapidly becoming the capital of US activity sports. Whether you come for the glitz and excitement or to make the most of such diverse terrain, one thing is certain—Vegas, once seen, is never forgotten.

The Luxor's Isis restaurant serves Continental food

WHAT'S IN THE SUBURBS

● A first-timer to Las Vegas will probably not venture beyond the environs of the Strip and Downtown, except perhaps for a trip out to the Grand Canyon. But beyond the central hub is a city like any other American metropolis, with schools, a university, parks, medical clinics, housing developments and some 500 churches. It is also a city with a growing ethnic population, each with its own distinctive neighborhood.

15

Las Vegas Then

Left to right: *Playing blackjack at El Rancho: The Rat Pack in Vegas; Folies Bergère at the Tropicana; nighttime at the Riviera*

EARLY BEGINNINGS

In prehistoric times the land on which the city stands was a marshy area that supported vigorous plant life, but the water eventually receded and the arid landscape we see today was created. However, underground water occasionally surfaced to nourish an oasis on the site where Vegas now stands, known at that time only to the area's Native Americans. Archeological finds just 10 miles (16km) northwest of Vegas have identified one of the oldest sites of human habitation in the United States. Items found at Tule Springs date from around 11,000 to 14,000 years ago.

1829 The spring at Las Vegas is discovered by a Mexican scout, Rafael Rivera, riding with a 60-strong trading party that had strayed from the Spanish Trail en route to Los Angeles.

1855 Mormon settlers build a fort at Las Vegas. They stay for three years, until Native American raids drive them out.

1905 On May 15, the railroad arrives, and trackside lots in what is now the Fremont Street area sell like hot cakes.

1910 Gambling is made illegal in the state of Nevada, sending the games underground.

1931 The Nevada legislature passes a bill to allow gambling, and El Rancho becomes the first casino to open in Las Vegas. Nevada remains the only state to allow casino gambling until 1976, when casinos are introduced to Atlantic City.

1940s A building boom expands Las Vegas and more casinos come to town, along with organized crime. Vegas is ruled by the Mafia for decades.

1946 The Flamingo, one of the foremost early casinos, opens its doors. It was financed by Benjamin "Bugsy" Siegel of the Meyer Lansky gang.

1959 The Tropicana Hotel buys the American rights to the Parisian Folies Bergère show—it's still running today.

1960s The Rat Pack (Frank Sinatra, Dean Martin, Sammy Davis Jr. et al.) come to Las Vegas, setting the pattern for superstar entertainment.

1966 Howard Hughes, pioneer aviator, billionaire and renowned recluse, takes up residence at the Desert Inn.

1967 The Nevada legislature approves a bill that allows publicly traded corporations to obtain gambling licenses. Legitimate money begins to loosen the Mafia's hold.

1976 Casino gambling is legalized in Atlantic City and, for the first time, Las Vegas has competition.

1990s Las Vegas begins to promote family attractions. Ever bigger, more fantastic architecture starts to dominate the Strip.

2001 Wayne Newton, "Mr Las Vegas," signs a lucrative 10-year contract with the Stardust Hotel.

2005 On May 15, Las Vegas celebrates its 100th birthday.

THE MORMON FORT

The first people to settle the area were not gamblers or casino owners—they were Mormons, who built a fort here in the mid-19th century. It became a welcome stopover for pioneers and traders on the Spanish Trail from Mexico to Los Angeles. The residents later turned to farming, but were driven out in 1858 when they'd had enough of the frequent raids by Native Americans. Today, the fort is open to the public, and you can see refurbished buildings and a re-created pioneer garden (⊠ 500 East Washington ☎ 702/486-3511 ⊙ Daily 8.30–3.30 📖 Inexpensive).

Time To Shop

Below: *The Forum shopping concourse*
Below right: *Fashion Show Mall*

Retail therapy in Vegas has soared in recent years, with an influx of designer and chic stores that has put the city firmly on the shopping map. With hundreds of well-known retailers and

PAWNSHOPS

The nature of the beast means Vegas attracts lots of pawnshops. Many are opposite gambling areas—open 24 hours—ready and waiting to unload desperate gamblers of their possessions for quick cash. Items that are not reclaimed within about 120 days are sold. You will discover all sorts of bizarre items at pawnshops, but jewelry, musical instruments and electrical equipment are the most common. Gone are the days of acquiring these items at rock-bottom prices, although you might pick up the odd little gem.

flagship department stores such as Neiman Marcus, Saks Fifth Avenue and Macy's, Vegas has joined other US cities in becoming a shopper's paradise. As shopping in Vegas mainly revolves around treading the elegant walkways of the numerous malls, it rather depends on how much money you have to spend and how far you are prepared to travel than on what you are looking to buy. If quaint individual shops are your forte, you're in the wrong city.

Most of the Strip hotels have their own shopping opportunities (➤ 72–73), some more spectacular than others, with The Forum at Caesars taking main stage. There is simply no other city in the world where you are able to shop under an artificial sky among Roman architecture and talking statues, journey between shops by gondola, or peruse exotic North African-style bazaars, all within a short distance of each other. Hotel malls in Vegas offer more than just great stores: All sorts of entertainment is lined up to amuse you as you shop, but this is reflected in the cost of the goods. There are other malls on the Strip not

attached to any particular hotel, such as the huge Fashion Show Mall (► 73), where you can browse through the boutiques while a fashion show takes place alongside.

Below: *For bargains, head to Vegas' outlet malls*
Below left: *Classy Via Bellagio*

Serious shoppers should venture a few blocks away from the Strip, where they will discover more vast malls filled with major retailers and specialist stores selling practical items at more realistic prices. Clothes range from daring and trendy to boutique exclusives, and the very latest in shoes, lingerie, jewelry and designer glasses complete a look suitable to hit the Vegas scene. True bargain hunters should head for one of the factory outlets (see panel ► 73), where top designer clothes, among other things, can be bought at 25–75 percent off. Items for the home, electronics and footwear are particularly good value.

At the other end of the scale from the classy boutiques are the endless souvenir shops along Las Vegas Boulevard, each selling the same mass-produced card decks and key rings. Every hotel also has a gift shop, with logo merchandise that exploits themes to the extreme, while casino gift shops are generally more elegant and expensive. Whether you shop on the Strip or in the malls farther afield, Las Vegas offers its own unique shopping experience.

THAT SPECIAL GIFT

Although Vegas is not known for one particular souvenir—apart from the kitsch in its gift shops—given the time and money you can buy almost anything here. Gambling merchandise abounds in every guise and quality leather jackets bearing logos are popular. Wine makes a safe gift as Vegas has the largest public collection of fine wines in the world. You might discover that unique collectible you've always wanted—a signed Michael Jordan basketball or auto-graphed Beatles poster. Precious jewels for sale in the city have included Ginger Rogers' engage-ment ring and the Moghul Emerald (the world's largest carved emerald), but these would break the bank—unless you strike it lucky of course.

Out and About

ORGANIZED SIGHTSEEING

Many Vegas-based tour companies offer trips from Vegas to wherever you want to go, but there are also plenty showing the best of the city sights. These tours can give you an insider's view on city attractions, along with a good overview and orientation, before you start exploring

Looking across the Grand Canyon from its South Rim

TOUR COMPANIES

ATV Action Tours, Inc.
180 Cassia Way, Suite 510, Henderson, NV 89014-6643
☎ 702/566-7400 or 888/288-5200;
www.actiontours.com

Coach USA
795 East Tropicana Avenue, Las Vegas, NV 89119 ☎ 702/735-4947 or 800/634-6579;
www.coachusa.com

Look Tours
2634 Airport Drive, Suite 103, North Las Vegas, NV 89032 ☎ 702/233-3792; www.looktours.com

Nitelife Tour Company
9413 Cedar Heights Avenue, Las Vegas, NV 89134 ☎ 800/695-5918;
www.vegasnitelife.com

Scenic Airlines
2705 Airport Drive, North Las Vegas, NV 89032
☎ 702/638-3300 or 800/634-6801;
www.scenic.com

Showtime Tours
1550 South Industrial Road, Las Vegas, NV 89102
☎ 702/895-9976 or 800/704-7011

independently. Nearly every hotel in Las Vegas has a sightseeing desk from where you can book tours.

If the tour bus approach doesn't appeal to you, there are all kinds of other options, including small-scale specialized tours with your own group of family or friends (try Creative Adventures ☎ 702/361-5565) or using a limousine to whisk you from place to place. Perhaps best of all, you can take to the skies in a helicopter for a bird's-eye view of the fantastic architecture and, on after-dark flights, the glittering lights. The Nitelife Tour Company's nightclub tours, also after dark, will transport you to the current most popular dance and Latin clubs. The company also offers a Las Vegas microbreweries tour.

The majority of the tour companies listed in the panel on the left run tours to nearby attractions, including the Valley of Fire State Park (► 62), Hoover Dam (► 48) and the Grand Canyon (► 49), and some offer adventure activities.

Walks

WET AND WILD

In the heat of the day, there's nothing like the sight and sound of water to have a cooling effect. This walk will take you along Las Vegas Boulevard South (the Strip), taking in all the best watery attractions—and some of the best architecture in Las Vegas—along the way.

The starting point is toward the southern end of Las Vegas Boulevard South at the Mandalay Bay resort. The big attraction here is the superb Shark Reef (➤ 26), which has all the water you could wish for—1.6 million gal (7.2 million liters) of it, to be precise. It is contained in a series of huge reconstructions of a variety of marine environments, with all the relevant marine life. The Back Reef Tunnel offers the nearest thing you'll get to immersing yourself completely (without getting wet, that is), and you'll be surrounded by many kinds of bright tropical fish and have close encounters with sleek sharks.

From here, walk north on the Strip as far as Harmon Avenue, where the Aladdin Hotel exudes the refreshing sound of cascading water from its 100ft (30m) waterfall. Go inside to wander along the exotic North African pier at Desert Passage (➤ 32), and stick around in order to experience the "Mediterranean thunderstorm" that is staged over its re-created bay every half-hour or so.

Back outside, cross the boulevard to the elegant Bellagio Hotel, which is home to the ultimate water attraction in the city. The palatial building is fronted by a huge lake where the best computerized fountain system in the world puts on a spectacular show at regular intervals through the day and night (➤ 34). You will see 20 million gal (90 million liters) of water being shot into the air, accompanied by a stirring soundtrack. Come back after dark to see the same thing with illuminations.

From the Bellagio, take the elevated walkway across Flamingo Road to Caesars Palace, where a massive aquarium forms part of the Atlantis

INFORMATION

Distance About 3.5 miles (5.5km)
Time Allow a day to see all the sights along the way
Start point Mandalay Bay
🚌 301, 302; Strip trolley
End point Circus Circus
🚌 301, 302; Strip trolley
🍴 Mon Ami Gabi at Paris Las Vegas (➤ 66); Hyakumi at Caesars Palace (➤ 67)

Top: *Mandalay Bay*
Above: *Bellagio's famous dancing fountains*

21

Walks

Looking north up the Strip

talking statue show. If you're there at the right time of day, you'll see divers inside the tank feeding the fish.

Next door to Caesars Palace is the Mirage (➤ 37). Its desert theme might not sound promising, but this is home to the delightful Dolphin Habitat. Walk through the hotel's shopping area and look for the door that will take you outside again to the resident bottlenose dolphins. Watch these playful creatures for a while, and maybe catch a splash or two, then retrace your steps back through the hotel. On the way out, take a look at the huge aquarium that sits behind the reception desk.

From the Mirage, walk north again on the Strip, until you get to the Treasure Island resort (there's a tram service, too, if you want to take some of the strain off your feet). Every hour, a full-size replica pirate ship comes into view on the bay to herald the start of the exciting *Sirens of Ti* show (➤ 54), set on the high seas.

Cross the boulevard again to the gorgeous Venetian hotel (➤ 38), where the cityscape of Venice has been replicated (without the erosion that plagues the original). Even St. Mark's Square has been reconstructed. Here you'll find a network of canals, lined by Venetian-style architecture and crossed by pretty little bridges. And you can while away some time on a relaxing gondola ride.

From the Venetian, go north again, cross over Spring Mountain Road, then cross to the other side of the boulevard to Circus Circus, home of the Adventuredome (➤ 42). This is a great place to end the walk. Not only are you out of the scorching sun, but you can really cool down by getting a soaking on the Rim Runner flume ride, then get blown dry with a high-speed ride on one of the indoor roller coasters.

Top: *Entertainers at the Venetian*

Above: *Vegas' Grand Canal*

22

Walks

LAS VEGAS ON A BUDGET

Surrounded by casino vaults stacked with cash and all the excesses that money can buy, you can still find plenty of excellent attractions that will cost you nothing or very little at all.

Start at the Excalibur (➤ 28), at the southern end of Las Vegas Boulevard South, where there are free shows at the Medieval Village. Cross the boulevard via the elevated walkway to the Tropicana, where from 11am you can catch one of the regular 20-minute "Air Play" productions. Daring acrobats, contortionists, singers and dancers perform in the air suspended above the casino floor.

Head north, crossing Tropicana Avenue on another overhead walkway, to reach the MGM Grand. Go into the casino to see the big cats in the Lion Habitat (➤ 30).

Walk north on the boulevard, calling in at M&M's World (➤ 58) for chocolate and at Desert Passage (➤ 32) for shopping. Cross the street to the Bellagio (➤ 34) to see the fountain show.

Take a cab from here along Flamingo Road to the Rio (➤ 87) to see its Masquerade Village, with the musical *Show in the Sky*.

Return down Flamingo Road to the boulevard and Caesars Palace, where a moving walkway will take you to The Forum and the animatronic talking statue show (➤ 35). Next door to Caesars, the Mirage has its free Volcano Show (➤ 37), after which you can see the *Sirens of Ti* cast do their stuff in Buccaneer Bay at Treasure Island (➤ 54).

Take a bus or cab (from outside Neiman Marcus) to Circus Circus for the circus acts on the second level, then cross Sahara Avenue to the Stratosphere for the free *Viva Las Vegas* show. End the day in Downtown with the spectacular Fremont Street Experience (➤ 46).

INFORMATION

Distance 4.5 miles (7km)
Time A day
Start point Excalibur
🚌 301, 302; Strip trolley
End point Fremont Street
🚌 301, 302; Strip trolley
🍴 NASCAR Café (➤ 43)

Below: *M&M's World*
Bottom: *The Fremont Street Experience by night*

Las Vegas by Night

Above and above right:
Vegas hots up after sunset

GAMING

Where else could you continually be refueled with free drinks as you take your chance at the blackjack table or wait for the roulette wheel to stop spinning? But be careful not to lose it all in one night. If you're not a serious player, the slot machines are lots of fun, too. Strolling through the casinos people-watching is another great way to pass the time—you'll see weary gamblers desperately trying to claw back some of their losses, and hear ecstatic cries of joy when their luck holds and the jangling of money when the slots pay out. Gaming is not just an after-dark activity (casinos stay open 24 hours), but it's late into the evening when things really heat up and big bucks are laid on the table.

Vegas really springs into action after the sun goes down, and some of the best attractions are to be found during the twilight hour. Night runs into day without you even noticing, as you soak up a pulsating nightlife scene like no other. Las Vegas is undoubtedly a great place to party.

From casino lounges to clubs, pubs and cocktail bars, the possibilities for a fun night out are endless. Numerous sizzling nightspots provide the chance to dance until dawn—and you're likely to spot a celebrity or two along the way. Ultra lounges are the latest trend, stylish spaces that attract a cutting-edge crowd, where DJs spin their vinyl but conversation takes priority. But this is Sin City, and there are several, not very well-concealed strip joints scattered throughout. These can, however, be disregarded among the sheer scale of everything else.

Las Vegas is world famous for its lavish stage entertainment, which incorporates unbelievable special effects. It has attracted some of the world's hottest superstars, from Pavarotti to the Rolling Stones. Shows vary from Broadway musicals and glittering stage extravaganzas to comedy and magic shows. Vegas also plays host to some of the world's biggest special events, such as world championship boxing matches. Beware, the top shows can be quite expensive and the most popular often need to be reserved well in advance. But the best show of all is free: Walk the Strip after dark and be treated to the amazing performance of thousands of flashing neon lights and fiber-optic signs.

LAS VEGAS'
top 25 sights

The sights are shown on the maps on the inside front cover and inside back cover, numbered **1**–**22** from south to north, except the excursions (**23**, **24** and **25**), which are arrowed off the map.

Shark Reef

HIGHLIGHTS

- Sharks up to 12ft (3.5m) long
- Back Reef Tunnel
- Talking to the naturalists
- Touch pool
- Golden crocodiles

INFORMATION

www.mandalaybay.com
- C9: Locator map A4
- Mandalay Bay, 3950 Las Vegas Boulevard South
- 702/632-7777
- Daily 10am–11pm; last admission 10pm
- Cafés and restaurants at Mandalay Bay
- 301, 302; Strip trolley
- Moderate
- King Tut's Tomb & Museum (➤ 27), Excalibur (➤ 28)
- Self-guiding audio tour included in price, with cards to help you identify fish

A hundred different species of shark, plus other magnificent aquatic creatures, can be encountered close up in the imaginatively re-created marine environments of this aquarium.

Massive tanks Shark Reef covers more than 91,000sq ft (8,450sq m) and its tanks—arranged in 14 main exhibits—contain an incredible 1.6 million gal (7.2 million liters) of mineral-rich reconstituted sea water. It's home to more than 2,000 species of marine creatures—not only the sharks, but also sea turtles, reptiles and fish.

The major exhibits The design of the exhibits is as entertaining as the inhabitants. In Treasure Bay, a sunken ship sits on the bed of a lagoon, circled by four kinds of shark. Shoals of snapper and jack dart around, in contrast to the laid-back gliding of the two green sea turtles. The experience of diving on a coral reef is re-created in the Back Reef Tunnel, whose water is full of bright tropical fish to the left, right and above you, and there is every probability of coming nose to nose with bonnethead sharks. Elsewhere, you will see rays skimming through the water or resting on the ocean floor.

Reptiles, amphibeans and jungle flora Rare golden crocodiles inhabit the Crocodile Habitat (the only place in the western hemisphere where you can see them), and in the Lizard Lounge there are huge water monitors up to 9ft (2.7m) in length. The Serpents and Dragons exhibit, separated from curious onlookers by only a pool of water, houses venomous snakes and the Australian Arowana dragon fish. The Temple exhibits offer a refreshing rain-forest experience, with mist on your skin, bird song and exotic flowers.

King Tut's Tomb & Museum

With its Egyptian theme and pyramid architecture, what else could the Luxor do but reproduce the glittering bounty of Egypt's most famous king and his renowned burial treasures?

"**I see wonderful things**" These were the words of British archeologist Howard Carter when he discovered the fabled tomb of Tutankhamun in 1922. It was the greatest archeological find of all time, the most intact tomb ever discovered in the Valley of the Kings (just outside the town of Luxor in Egypt) and took 10 years to excavate. In contrast, the Luxor hotel replicated the tomb in its Pharaoh Pavilion in just six months. Even so, this is no tacky imitation. The finds exhibited in the museum were faithfully created by craftsmen in Egypt, using traditional methods and tools that were employed thousands of years ago, and incorporating authentic materials such as gold leaf and precious pigments. It is the only exhibit of its kind outside of Egypt.

Museum tour It takes 15 minutes to follow the self-guiding audio tour of the museum, but it constitutes a breathtaking quarter-hour. The entire layout of King Tutankhamun's tomb has been exactly re-created under the direction of renowned Egyptologist Dr. Omar Mabreuck, who supervised the 50-strong team. The focus is, of course, the sarcophagus of the young king and the illustrious guardian statues that watched over his last resting place. The original tomb consisted of nine outer cases protecting the mummified remains, and the innermost one was made of solid gold. There are also beautifully crafted figurines and wall paintings, and subdued lighting casts an atmospheric golden glow over the entire exhibit. There's a shop at the exit with some exquisite pieces for sale.

HIGHLIGHTS

- The golden tomb
- Replica gold-plated sarcophagus
- The museum shop, where authentic Egyptian art is on sale

INFORMATION

www.luxor.com
- C9: Locator map A4
- Luxor, 3900 Las Vegas Boulevard South
- 702/262-4555
- Sun–Thu 9am–11pm, Fri, Sat 9am–midnight
- Cafés and restaurants at Luxor
- 301, 302; Strip trolley
- Inexpensive
- Shark Reef (▶ 26), Excalibur (▶ 28), New York–New York (▶ 31)
- Self guiding audio tour is independent of other visitors so you can take it any time you choose

Excalibur

HIGHLIGHTS

- *Tournament of Kings*
- Court Jester's Stage
- Merlin's Magic Motion Rides

INFORMATION

www.excalibur-casino.com

☩ C9: Locator map A3

✉ 3850 Las Vegas Boulevard South

☎ 702/597-7777. Merlin's Magic Motion Machine: 702/597-7084

◉ Court Jester's Stage: daily 11–7.30. *Tournament of Kings*: daily 6 and 8.30pm; advance reservations recommended. Merlin's Magic Motion Machine: Sun–Thu 11–10, Fri, Sat 10am–midnight

🍴 Several cafés and restaurants

🚌 301, 302; Strip trolley

⚔ *Tournament of Kings*: very expensive. Merlin's Magic Motion Machine: inexpensive

🔁 Shark Reef (► 26), King Tut's Tomb & Museum (► 27), New York–New York (► 31)

❷ You must be at least 42in (1.06m) tall to go on the motion simulator rides

All the romance and excitement of legendary medieval Europe is re-created at this sparkling castle-shaped hotel, with exciting special effects, sword fights, jousting and jugglers.

Camelot Cross the drawbridge and you enter a world where technology meets the legend of King Arthur. Inside the stone walls, stained glass and heraldic shields set the scene, and strolling performers dressed in costumes enhance the atmosphere. That said, it's all a bit cheesy, but kids love it.

Medieval Village An escalator transports you to the second floor, where you are greeted by a fire-breathing dragon. The main stage presents free shows, including juggling, puppetry and story-telling. On the lower level at the Fantasy Faire Midway, there are traditional carnival attractions, state-of-the-art video games and Merlin's Magic Motion simulator rides. Shops sell medieval-style merchandise, and there are several themed restaurants to choose from.

Tournament of Kings This enthralling show revolves around highly skilled stunts—often on horseback—high-tech special effects, wonderful costumes and a stirring musical score. King Arthur and his knights play host to other monarchs across Europe. There's a procession, followed by traditional medieval games of skill, agility, might and endurance. But when the evil Mordred attacks, amid burning fires and accompanied by a dragon, the clash of swords begins. The victor is presented with Excalibur by Merlin and the show ends with more festivities. While pulling apart their chicken dinner with greasy hands, the audience is involved in partisan support during the jousting.

Liberace Museum

Outrageous, lavish, ostentatious and dazzling—a testament to bad taste and kitsch. This statement could easily be used as a slogan for Las Vegas city, but here it refers to just one collection, the incredible Liberace Musem.

Setting the scene From the moment you see the fluorescent pink entrance sign, you are drawn into the world of one of the most extraordinary entertainers of the 20th century. This shrine to the legend of "Mr Showmanship" is as outrageous as Liberace himself. The museum, the legacy of the world's highest paid musician and pianist, was founded by Liberace in 1977 as a nonprofit organization. On show are vintage pianos and cars, the most exuberant costumes, glitzy jewelry and a host of memorabilia.

From classical beginnings Born in the US in 1919 of Italian/Polish parents, Wladziu Liberace had a classical training and made his debut with the Chicago Symphony at the age of 14. He went on to become well known on the nightclub circuit and on television, and in 1955 he opened at the Riviera as the highest-paid entertainer in the city's history. Liberace then took the world by storm, his flamboyant style always attracting attention. He died in 1987.

Antiques to kitsch To the rippling tones of Liberace's keyboard artistry you can view an amazing collection of pianos, including rare antiques. Check out the rhinestone-encrusted Baldwin grand and Liberace's favorite, covered entirely in glittering mirror squares. See the superb bejeweled Rolls-Royces, sequined, feathered and rhinestone-studded costumes, and a glittering array of jewelry, including the trademark candelabra ring. Seeing is believing.

HIGHLIGHTS

- Concert piano collection
- Rolls-Royce collection
- Costumes, including a black diamond mink cape and the famous red, white and blue hot-pants suit
- Candelabra ring
- Precious stone collection
- Re-creation of Palm Springs bedroom

INFORMATION

www.liberace.org
- G9: Locator map C3
- 1775 East Tropicana Avenue, at Spencer
- 702/798-5595
- Mon–Sat 10–5, Sun noon–4
- 201
- Moderate
- Lion Habitat (➤ 30)

Lion Habitat

HIGHLIGHTS

- Having a photo taken with one of the cubs
- Watching the trainers interact with the lions

INFORMATION

www.mgmgrand.com

- D8: Locator map B3
- MGM Grand, 3799 Las Vegas Boulevard South
- 702/891-7777
- Daily 11–10
- Cafés and restaurants at MGM Grand
- MGM Grand
- 301, 302; Strip trolley
- Free
- Liberace Museum (➤ 29), Desert Passage (➤ 32)

This is a remarkable place, where you can get up close to magnificent big cats in the happy knowledge that their stay in the enclosure will be only slightly longer than yours.

A temporary sojourn Anyone who has qualms about wild animals being caged for human entertainment can rest assured that the lions are brought here for just a short time from their spacious home outside the city. They belong to animal trainer Keith Evans, who makes the trip three times a day to ensure that no cat is in the enclosure for longer than six hours.

Surrounded by lions The three-level structure, reaching a height of more than 35ft (10m), is similar in concept to the walk-through tunnels you'll find in big aquariums. You will see the animals close up, and can study their every move with perfect clarity as they prowl on either side and even stride across the tunnel roof above your head—and all that separates you is a thick layer of the toughest strengthened glass available. The Lion Habitat has been laid out to resemble the natural landscape the cats would know in the wild, including indigenous foliage, rocks, four separate waterfalls and a pond.

Raised in captivity One of the most famous lions of all time was Metro, whose roar announced every MGM Studio production. Three of his descendants—Goldie, Metro and Baby Lion—are among the collection of more than two dozen big cats, all of which have been raised in captivity by Evans and his wife. Their 8-acre (3ha) estate provides a spacious permanent home for the lions, but there will be up to five at a time on view in the enclosure, along with Evans himself and other trainers.

New York–New York

See the sights of the Big Apple in a fraction of the time needed to explore the real thing. The Statue of Liberty, Brookyn Bridge, the Chrysler Building—they are all here.

New York in miniature Standing 47 floors high, this resort hotel claims to be the tallest in Nevada. The New York skyline is depicted through scaled-down replicas—about one-third of the actual size—of famous city landmarks. The Statue of Liberty keeps watch over the Strip side by side with skyscrapers such as the Empire State Building and a 300ft-long (91m) version of the Brooklyn Bridge.

Manhattan Express A thrilling roller coaster twists, loops and dives at speeds of up to 60mph (97kph) around the skyscrapers to a height of 203ft (62m). Your whole world literally turns upside down and inside out when the train drops 144ft (44m). This ride was the first ever to introduce the "heartline" twist and dive move, where riders experience weightlessness—the train rolls 180 degrees, suspending its passengers 86ft (26m) above the casino roof, before taking a sudden dive.

Behind the scenes The hotel's art deco lobby is set against representations of Times Square, Little Italy and Wall Street, and the casino is modeled on Central Park. A selection of restaurants and shops also follows the theme. Upstairs, the Coney Island Emporium re-creates the atmosphere of an early-1900s amusement park alongside the latest video technology. ESPN Zone is a sports-themed entertainment and dining complex, where a huge arena provides interactive and competitive games, and you can view sports on 14ft (4m) screens.

HIGHLIGHTS

- Manhattan Express
- Statue of Liberty
- Brooklyn Bridge
- ESPN Zone

INFORMATION

www.nynyhotelcasino.com
- C8: Locator map A3
- 3790 Las Vegas Boulevard South
- 702/740-6969
- Manhattan Express: Sun–Thu 11–11, Fri, Sat 11–midnight. ESPN Zone: Mon–Thu 11.30am–12.30am, Fri 11.30am–1.30am, Sat 11am–1.30am, Sun 11am–12.30am. Coney Island Emporium: Mon–Thu 8am–midnight, Fri–Sun 8am–2am
- Several cafés and restaurants
- MGM Grand
- 301, 302; Strip trolley
- Manhattan Express: moderate
- Excalibur (▶ 28), King Tut's Tomb & Museum (▶ 27)
- You must be 54in (1.38m) to ride the roller coaster

Desert Passage

DID YOU KNOW?

● At the time of publication, the Aladdin had been bought by Planet Hollywood, though no significant changes were predicted in the near future.

INFORMATION

www.desertpassage.com
➕ C8: Locator map A3
✉ Aladdin Resort, 3667 Las Vegas Boulevard South
☎ 702/866-0703
🕓 Sun–Thu 10am–11pm, Fri, Sat 10am–midnight
🍴 Several cafés and restaurants
Ⓑ Bally's/Paris
🚌 301, 302; Strip trolley
♿ Free
↔ Lion Habitat (➤ 30), Paris Las Vegas (➤ 33), Bellagio (➤ 34)
❓ You will walk about 1 mile (1.6km) if you want to see the whole complex, so wear comfortable shoes

A North African bazaar and a busy trading port, with all the exciting sights and sounds of Tangier or Marrakesh, lend an exotic slant to this modern shopping and entertainment complex.

Shopping with a difference Make no mistake, this is a shopping mall, with 130 retailers and more than a dozen restaurants, but it couldn't be farther from an ordinary retail experience. Here you can relive the experiences of merchants on the ancient trade and spice routes as you browse the unusual items in the authentic-looking marketplace. Architectural historians devised the mountainside setting, with its Moorish arches and iron grilles, and regional culturists were consulted about the type and quality of the goods on offer. These include genuine antiques from the region, glazed ceramics and other craft items. Needless to say, there is every opportunity to sample North African cuisine in the restaurants.

On the harborfront Desert Passage is also home to the bustling Merchant's Harbor, complete with the sounds of lapping waves and deckhands rushing back and forth from the full-size European freighter, 155ft (47m) long, that is moored on the dockside. The architecture lining the quay blends colonial French with the gleaming whitewashed buildings that distinguish the area, and the atmosphere is exciting and full of local character.

Stormy weather At regular intervals you will hear the rumble of distant thunder as a "Mediterranean storm" begins to brew. Clouds gather, a cooling breeze starts up and a gentle rain falls on the harbor, although you won't need an umbrella from your viewpoint on the shore.

Paris Las Vegas

Striving to capture the Parisian style of "gay Paree," this hotel has succeeded in creating fine likenesses of the Eiffel Tower, Arc de Triomphe, Paris Opera House and Le Louvre.

Joie de vivre This eye-catching resort may not be the real thing, but a characteristic exuberance is reflected in thoughtful touches like singing breadmen on bikes dressed in striped shirts, red scarves and berets, and a joyful *"Bonjour!"* from roving street performers.

Eiffel Tower Experience The symbol of this hotel is the 525ft (160m) Eiffel Tower (half the size of the original), which was re-created using Gustav Eiffel's blueprints. A glass elevator takes you to the observation deck on the 50th floor for spectacular views of Las Vegas and the surrounding mountains—especially impressive at dusk when the Strip lights up. Eleven floors above the Strip is the sophisticated and pricey Eiffel Tower restaurant and bar. Three of the tower's four legs plunge into the casino below.

Le Boulevard Don't miss this French-style shopping boulevard, which gives you a taste of one of Europe's most lively cities. The 31,000sq ft (2,880sq m) of retail heaven connect Paris Las Vegas to Bally's, the hotel's sister property. Amid winding alleyways and cobbled streets, the ornate facades conceal elegant French boutiques, shops and restaurants. Weathered brickwork and brass lamps give an authentic rustic finish, and window boxes overflowing with bright blooms complete the Parisian picture. The very French Le Theatre des Arts plays host to the not-so-very-French London smash hit stage show *We Will Rock You* (➤ 54), based on the story of rock band Queen.

DID YOU KNOW?

The Eiffel Tower in Paris:
- Overall height 1,050ft (320m)
- 1,655 steps to the top
- 2.5 million rivets hold the tower together
- 59 tons (60 tonnes) of paint are needed to repaint it
- 9,840 tons (10,000 tonnes) in weight
- 6,230,050 people visited in 2004

INFORMATION

www.parislasvegas.com
- C7: Locator map A3
- 3655 Las Vegas Boulevard South
- 702/946-7000
- Eiffel Tower Experience: daily 10am–1am (weather permitting)
- Several cafés and restaurants
- Bally's/Paris
- 301, 302; Strip trolley
- Eiffel Tower Experience: moderate
- Desert Passage (➤ 32), Bellagio (➤ 34)

Bellagio

INFORMATION

www.bellagio.com

- C7: Locator map A3
- ✉ 3600 Las Vegas Boulevard South
- ☎ 702/693-7111
- ⊙ Fountains: Mon–Fri 3pm–midnight; Sat, Sun noon–midnight; shows every half-hour to 8pm then every 15 mins (dependent on weather conditions)
- ⏹ Several cafés and restaurants
- ⊛ Bally's/Paris
- ⊟ 301, 302; Strip trolley
- ⊛ Fountains free
- ⬌ Desert Passage (► 32); Paris Las Vegas (► 33); Caesars Palace & The Forum (► 35)
- ❓ No under-18s are allowed in the Bellagio unless accompanied by a registered guest

The Italianate image for this $1.6 billion hotel, deemed to be one of the most opulent resorts in the world, was inspired by the village of Bellagio on the shores of Italy's Lake Como.

A touch of class An 8-acre (3ha) man-made lake at the front of the hotel sets the stage for the elegance, art and grandeur that awaits you inside. The dazzling front lobby has an 18ft (5.5m) ceiling with a chandelier of glass flowers suspended in the middle, designed by glass sculptor Dale Chihuly. All this splendor is enhanced by the wonderful botanical garden, set under a glass atrium.

Fountains at the Bellagio During the choreographed, computer-controlled fountain show, millions of gallons of water are sprayed to heights of 240ft (73m) above the hotel's massive lake. The system uses individually programmed water jets and atomizing nozzles that create an atmospheric fog on the lake; some jets can change the direction of the water, giving a dancing effect. The show is further enhanced by the integrated illumination that comes into play after dark, and by the audio system, with music ranging from Pavarotti to Sinatra.

So much more The Bellagio is very proud of its Gallery of Fine Art (► 56), and its magnificent theater was styled after the Paris Opera specifically for Cirque du Soleil's *"O"* (see panel ► 52), in which a cast of synchronized swimmers, divers, contortionists, trapeze artists and others perform on an amazing liquid stage. The extravagant glass-enclosed Via Bellagio shopping mall (► 72) houses a collection of designer boutiques and shops, and the hotel also boasts the coveted restaurant Picasso (► 66).

Caesars Palace & The Forum

So you are in Las Vegas, but the thing you most want to do is spend a day shopping for Italian designer chic surrounded by the historic buildings of ancient Rome? No problem. It's all right here at Caesars Palace.

Classical architecture Visit this superb complex and you could easily believe yourself transported into the Italian capital, amid architecture that spans the period from 300BC to AD1700. The grounds are filled with reproductions of Roman statues, marble columns and colonnades, and toga-clad cocktail waitresses and costumed centurions contribute to the atmosphere.

Short days At the heart of things is the phenomenal shopping concourse, The Forum. Wander in and out of such stores as Versace and Armani, with an artificial sky overhead that gives the illusion that 24 hours have passed in just one hour. And when fatigue sets in, there's a big selection of restaurants within the complex.

Daily shows Every hour the Festival of Fountains springs into action, when statues come to life, special effects kick in, and you are entertained by gods and other characters from Roman mythology. In the Roman Great Hall, more special effects, plus animatronics, fire, water and smoke, combine to portray the struggle to rule Atlantis, with the backdrop of a massive marine aquarium housing sharks, stingrays and more than 100 other species. The 4,000-seat Colosseum hosts big-name shows, including Céline Dion's spectacular, *A New Day…* (▶ 52). Other attractions include a 3-D IMAX motion simulator where super-sized three-dimensional images and sound systems offer a unique experience.

HIGHLIGHTS

- Marine aquarium
- Shops in The Forum
- Festival of Fountains
- Marble statuary and fountains

INFORMATION

www.caesars.com

- C7. Locator map A3
- 3570 Las Vegas Boulevard South
- 702/731-7110. The Forum/ *Race for Atlantis*: 702/733-9000
- The Forum and *Race for Atlantis*: Sun–Thu 10am–11pm, Fri, Sat 10am–midnight
- Several cafés and restaurants
- Flamingo/Caesars
- 301, 302; Strip trolley
- *Race for Atlantis*: moderate
- Bellagio (▶ 34)
- Free behind-the-scenes tours at 1.15 and 5.15pm

Imperial Palace Auto Collections

Top: *1930 Duesenberg*
Below: *1933 Pierce Arrow*

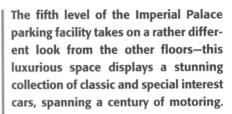

**The fifth level of the Imperial Palace
parking facility takes on a rather different look from the other floors—this
luxurious space displays a stunning
collection of classic and special interest
cars, spanning a century of motoring.**

Plush parking You could easily spend hours
here, in what is one of the finest and largest
automobile collections in the world. When it
opened in 1981 the collection had 200 vehicles;
since then, this number has increased to an
impressive 750. There are gleaming examples
of all those classics that generations of drivers
have yearned for, there are rare and exclusive
models, and there are cars that represent landmarks in vehicle construction and technology.
A significant acquisition for the exhibition here
is the world's largest collection of Model J.
Duesenbergs.

Famous and infamous owners Some of the vehicles that hold the greatest fascination are those
that are noteworthy because of the people who
drove them. You might see Marilyn Monroe's
pink 1955 Lincoln Capri covertible, an armor-
plated 1939 Mercedes-Benz used by Adolph
Hitler, and cars owned by Al Capone, Elvis
Presley, Benito Mussolini and James Cagney.
There's no certainty about what will be on show
because this is not exactly a straightforward
museum, and the
collection is not nec-
essarily a permanent
one. All of the
exhibits are for sale,
and serious buyers
may well be among
your fellow browsers
on the lot.

The Mirage

There is nothing so fascinating as the power of nature, and to watch the Mirage's simulated volcano erupt or get close up with the magnificent wildlife is a highlight of anyone's day.

Tropical delights This Polynesian-style resort is appropriately fronted by cascading waterfalls, tropical foliage and an imitation volcano. As you enter the lobby you can't miss the huge coral-reef aquarium stocked with tropical fish, and if you venture farther in you will discover a lush rain forest under a large atrium.

Eruptions to order You can wait years for a real volcano to create its spectacle, but here, in front of the Mirage, you can set your watch by it. The spectacular two-minute shows start with a rumbling sound, then a fog swirls around and a column of smoke and fire shoots 100ft (30m) into the sky. The computer-controlled show includes 34 gas-fueled special effects, with real flames on the water of the lagoon, and state-of-the-art lighting techniques. Arrive in good time so you can stake out a front-row position.

Wonderful wildlife Out the back is Siegfried & Roy's Secret Garden (the performers' stage show was suspended in 2003 after Roy was mauled by one of their big cats). Here, they re-create a jungle habitat that is home to such creatures as royal white tigers, white lions, Bengal tigers, snow leopards and an Asian elephant. The nearby Dolphin Habitat provides a happy and nuturing environment for nine Atlantic bottlenose dolphins. Watch them frolic above water or below from the viewing gallery, and learn more about marine mammals on a 15-minute tour. The dolphins breed regularly, so you might be lucky enough to see a baby at play.

HIGHLIGHTS

- Volcanic eruption
- Secret Garden and white tigers
- Dolphin Habitat

INFORMATION

www.themirage.com

✚ C7: Locator map A3

✉ 3400 Las Vegas Boulevard South

☎ 702/791-7111. Secret Garden: 702/791-7188

◷ Volcanic eruption: every 15 mins dusk–midnight. Secret Garden/Dolphin Habitat: Mon–Fri 11–5.30, Sat, Sun 10–5.30 (hours vary seasonally)

🍴 Several cafés and restaurants

🚌 301, 302; Strip trolley

💲 Volcanic eruption: free. Secret Garden/Dolphin Habitat: moderate

↔ Imperial Palace Auto Collections (➤ 36), the Venetian (➤ 38), Guggenheim Hermitage Museum (➤ 39), Madame Tussaud's Celebrity Encounter (➤ 40)

The Venetian

INFORMATION

www.venetian.com

✚ C7: Locator map A3

✉ 3355 Las Vegas Boulevard South

☎ 702/414-1000. Grand Canal Shoppes/gondola ride: 702/414-4500

◉ Grand Canal Shoppes: Sun–Thu 10am–11pm, Fri, Sat 10am–midnight. Gondola ride: Sun–Thu 10am–11pm, Fri, Sat 10am–midnight; last ride leaves 15 mins before closing

🍴 Several cafés and restaurants

🚋 301, 302; Strip trolley

✋ Gondola ride: moderate

⟷ The Mirage (► 37), Guggenheim Hermitage Museum (► 39), Madame Tussaud's Celebrity Encounter (► 40)

❓ Reservations for gondola rides must be made in person at the loading dock

Owner Sheldon Adelson's spectacular replica of Venice has gone a long way to catch the flavor of this most romantic city. But at the same time it has retained all the glitz and pizzazz expected from Las Vegas.

Most authentic This $1.5 billion resort is one of the city's most aesthetically pleasing properties. The ornate lobby has domed and vaulted ceilings, exquisite marble floors and reproductions of frescoes framed in gold. An excellent take on Venice, it has its own 1,200ft-long (365m) Grand Canal—the real one extends 2.5 miles (4km). The waterway meanders under arched bridges, including the Rialto, and past the vibrant piazza of St. Mark's Square and other familiar Venice landmarks. In the casino hang the works of artists Tiepolo, Tintoretto and Titian. The Venetian is also home to Madame Tussaud's interactive wax museum (► 40) and the Guggenheim Hermitage Museum (► 39).

Gondola ride From St. Mark's you can board a gondola and be carried down the Grand Canal to the soothing sound of water lapping against the sides; there is even a wedding gondola if you want to take the plunge. Everything looks particularly spectacular at dusk, when the spirit of Venice is really captured.

Time to shop The Grand Canal Shoppes mall lines an indoor cobblestoned plaza alongside the canal and is linked by walkways. There are fine restaurants and interesting shops behind faux facades, ranging from Davidoff cigars and Mikimoto pearls to Jimmy Choo shoes and chic jewelry stores such as Choper. Strolling opera singers perform Italian arias while various other street entertainers do their thing.

Guggenheim Hermitage Museum

When the Guggenheim Hermitage Museum opened in September 2001 it added a new dimension to Las Vegas, an outstanding cultural institution that would offer a stimulating art exhibition to a new breed of tourist.

A dignified approach It would have been too easy for the Venetian hotel to continue its theme of replicating Venice with a re-creation of the Guggenheim's canalside modern art gallery in that city. Happily, they have instead created a serious art space, designed by architect Rem Koolhaas, in which to display the Guggenheim Foundation's wonderful collection, including classic works from Russia's State Hermitage Museum in St. Petersburg. These are set off to perfection against the dark, textured walls, within a free-standing structure inside the hotel. It is a venture that has broadened the appeal of this popular destination, while maintaining the dignity of the cultural institution.

The collection Solomon R. Guggenheim had a mission to educate the public about the type of art that drew upon pure artistic invention, and set about putting examples of abstract art on public display. The Guggenheim Foundation's extensive collection is based around this nonobjective form, but contains examples of all kinds of modern art, spanning the late 19th century to the present day, and including impressionism and abstract expressionism. It contains works by all the major artists who have played a significant role in the development of artistic style, and is particularly strong on post-war contemporary art. The Hermitage Museum in Las Vegas is most definitely an A-list gallery, on a par with New York's Metropolitan Museum of Art and the Louvre in Paris.

DID YOU KNOW?

- There are four more Guggenheim museums in addition to this one in Las Vegas, all part of the Guggenheim Foundation
- The New York museum opened in 1959, while the Venice collection was donated by Peggy Guggenheim and opened in 1951. The spectacular Bilbao gallery in Spain and the Deutsche Guggenheim in Berlin, a joint venture between the bank and the museum, both opened their doors in 1997

INFORMATION

www.guggenheimlasvegas.org
✚ C7: Locator map A3
▣ The Venetian, 3355 Las Vegas Boulevard South
☎ 702/414-2440
🕐 Daily 9.30–8.30
🍴 Several cafés and restaurants at the Venetian
🚌 301, 302; Strip trolley
♿ Moderate
🔄 The Mirage (► 37), the Venetian (► 38), Madame Tussaud's Celebrity Encounter (► 40)

Madame Tussaud's Celebrity Encounter

HIGHLIGHTS

- "The King in Concert"
- "Marry Clooney"
- Behind-the-scenes tour

INFORMATION

www.madametussaudslv.com

+ C6/7: Locator map A3
- ✉ The Venetian, 3355 Las Vegas Boulevard South
- ☎ 702/862-7800
- 🕐 Daily 10–10 (hours vary seasonally)
- 🍴 Several cafés and restaurants at the Venetian
- 🚌 301, 302; Strip trolley
- 💵 Expensive
- ↔ The Mirage (➤ 37), the Venetian (➤ 38), Guggenheim Hermitage Museum (➤ 39)

It is fitting that Madame Tussaud's first foray into the United States should be in Las Vegas, a magnet for both the biggest showbiz personalities and the most ardent celebrity-spotters.

Making an impression Madame Tussaud's is the world leader when it comes to making realistic likenesses in wax of the rich, famous and infamous. The secret is that they take an impression from the real person, rather than simply use an artist's sculpture, so every detail is absolutely spot on. Though this can be a rather claustrophobic experience (Napoleon was famously freaked out by it), new celebrities regard it as at least one of the signs that they have made it in the business. Being removed from a Madame Tussaud's display can be quite a blow to the ego.

Las Vegas legends Not surprisingly, pride of place here goes to the superstars who have made their mark in Vegas—Wayne Newton, Tony Bennett, Engelbert Humperdinck, Tom Jones and the Rat Pack, to name just a few. Among more than 100 other masterfully produced figures is an international cast of movie and TV stars, icons from the music world and sport's big achievers.

Interactive experience Some exhibits allow you to interact with the famous models by taking part in a scenario, such as becoming the next "Pop Idol" by performing in front of critic Simon Cowell—but be prepared to take his insults on the chin. Or chance your luck alongside Ben Affleck in "Celebrity Poker." The highlight for every female must be the "Marry Clooney" exhibit, where you put on a wedding gown and walk down the aisle with George himself—in your dreams!

Star Trek: The Experience

Enter (as boldly as you like) into the spirit of this out-of-this-world attraction and you'll have enormous fun. Dedicated Trekkies will, of course, find themselves in absolute heaven.

Beam me up There can be only one way to begin a visit to Star Trek: The Experience—yes, you really are beamed aboard a re-creation of the USS *Enterprise*, to be greeted on the bridge by various crew members. Here you are issued with your mission, then escorted into the TurboLift and along the Grand Corridor to the Shuttle Bay to board a 27-seat spacecraft. By now you might have realized that it's all been a big build-up for an exciting high-speed simulator journey through the distant galaxies. If you don't fancy this stomach-churning chase, there is the *Borg Invasion 4-D*—a 3-D film with state-of-the-art audiovisual effects.

History of the Future Museum Back on terra firma, but still quite far removed from reality, you can have a look around this huge collection of the actual props and memorabilia used in the nine *Star Trek* movies and four TV series. There are crew uniforms, some of the costumes and makeup that created the various weird and wonderful alien beings, special effects, stage props and weaponry, totaling more than 200 items.

Deep Space Nine Promenade This is a slightly different retail space with a range of *Star Trek*-themed stuff to buy, from props and collectibles to crafted jewelry and art. You can kit the family out in *Star Trek* uniforms or buy celebrity cardboard cut-outs. When you need refreshment, the Quark's Bar & Restaurant menu includes "hamborger," "flaming ribs of Targ," "glop on a stick" and "final frontier" desserts.

HIGHLIGHTS

- *Borg Invasion 4-D*
- Klingon Encounter
- Museum exhibits

INFORMATION

www.startrekexp.com
- ➕ E5/6: Locator map B2
- ✉ Las Vegas Hilton, 3000 Paradise Road
- ☎ 702/697-8750
- 🕐 Daily 11.30–9.30 (hours vary seasonally)
- 🍴 Restaurant and bar
- 🚌 Las Vegas Hilton
- 🚌 108
- 🎟 Combo ticket: expensive
- ↔ Circus Circus (➤ 42)
- ❓ You must be at least 42in (1.06m) tall to go on the motion simulator ride

Circus Circus

The circus has come to town. In fact, it arrived here on the Strip in 1968 when Circus Circus opened its doors to provide the city with its first gaming concern offering family entertainment.

Roll up, roll up At first there were no hotel rooms at Circus Circus, only a casino and the world's biggest permanent circus tent. Today, however, around 1,500 guest rooms are stacked in towers behind the first-floor casino, while the upper floor has a wealth of carnival attractions and arcade games surrounding a circus arena. Acrobats, trapeze artists, aerialists and clowns are just some of the acts from around the globe that perform daily under the big top.

Undercover thrills In 1993 the Adventuredome was added, said to be the biggest indoor theme park in the country, covering about 5 acres (2ha) beneath an enormous glass dome. The main thrill rides (for the very brave) include the Canyon Blaster, a massive double-loop, double-corkscrew roller coaster that achieves a top speed of 55mph (88kph); Chaos, which hurls its passengers in all directions as it speeds on its unpredictable course; and the Inverter, which literally turns your world upside down. If you enjoy getting very wet, head for the Rim Runner, a waterborne ride that includes a breathtaking plunge. Equally thrilling is the IMAX Ridefilm Cineplex, with high-speed motion simulation and startling computer-generated images.

Gentler fun There are less stressful rides and activities, too, to please all ages. These include team laser tag and a climbing wall, while younger children will love the carousels, bumper cars and miniature golf.

DID YOU KNOW?

- The temperature in the Adventuredome is kept at a constant 72°F (22°C)
- The Rim Runner ride and waterfall circulate 600,000 gal (2.72 million liters) of water
- The tallest mountain peak in the Adventuredome is 140ft (43m) high

INFORMATION

www.circuscircus.com

🔲 D5: Locator map B2

✉ 2880 Las Vegas Boulevard South

☎ 702/734-0410. Adventuredome: 702/794-3939

🎡 Midway Circus Acts: every half-hour 11am–midnight. Adventuredome: Mon–Thu 10–6, Fri, Sat 10am–midnight, Sun 10–8 (hours may vary seasonally)

🍴 Several cafés and restaurants

🚌 301, 302; Strip trolley

🎢 Adventuredome: free admission, charge for rides; daily pass expensive

↔ Star Trek: The Experience (► 41), NASCAR Café & Speed: The Ride (► 43)

❓ Height restrictions may apply on some Adventuredome rides

NASCAR Café & Speed: The Ride

People are racing to this motor-sport themed café, with its state-of-the-art simulators, real stock cars, 3-D racing movies and the fastest roller coaster in the world winding in and out of the building.

NASCAR Café To call it a café hardly gives an accurate impression of this massive venue and its exciting attractions. But café it is, with 400 seats and an all-American menu. In addition, though, there are some amazing motor-racing exhibits, focusing on "Carzilla," the world's largest stock car. The upper level has eight regular-size stock cars suspended from the ceiling in racing formation, and there are about a dozen more cars around the place, plus lots of other racing exhibits. While you munch on your lunch you can watch staff carry out a 20-second pitstop and see NASCAR news and driver profiles on giant screens. Would-be racing drivers can then try out their skills on the Las Vegas Cyber Speedway, where model stock cars are mounted on hydraulic bases with plenty of controls to personalize the ride. Those who want to feel the thrill of the race without stepping in a car should check out the 3-D movie experience.

Speed: The Ride Inside the café you can climb aboard this roller coaster, the fastest in town, going from 0 to 40mph (64kph) in about two seconds, then accelerating to 70mph (113kph) as it bursts out of the building onto Sahara Avenue. The ride features a plunge through a tunnel, an exhilarating loop, a quick trip through the Sahara marquee and a stop at 224ft (68m) above ground...and then you cover the whole track again in reverse. This is not for the fainthearted, and is perhaps best experienced before you eat lunch!

HIGHLIGHTS

- Meet the racing drivers when they are in town
- Cyber Speedway

INFORMATION

www.saharahotelandcasino. com

✛ E5. Locator map B2

✉ Sahara, 2535 Las Vegas Boulevard South

☎ 702/737-2111

🕐 Cyber Speedway: Mon–Thu noon–9, Fri noon–10, Sat 11–10, Sun 11–9. Speed: Sun–Thu 10–10, Fri, Sat 10am–1am

🚇 Sahara

🚌 301, 302; Strip trolley

🎟 Day pass: moderate

🔄 Circus Circus (➤ 47)

❓ You must be at least 54in (1.37m) tall to ride the Cyber Speedway

Stratosphere Tower

HIGHLIGHTS

- The view from the observation deck
- A gourmet meal in the Top of the World restaurant
- The thrill rides

INFORMATION

www.stratospherehotel.com

🔲 E4: Locator map B2

✉ 2000 Las Vegas Boulevard South

☎ 702/380-7777

🕐 Rides: Sun–Thu 10am–1am, Fri, Sat 10am–2am (hours vary seasonally)

🍴 Top of the World restaurant; snack bar

🚌 301, 302

🎢 Tower: moderate (no charge if you have a restaurant reservation). Individual rides including admission to tower: moderate. Multiride ticket: expensive

🔁 Downtown (► 45), Fremont Street Experience (► 46)

❓ You must be at least 48in (1.22m) tall to ride the High Roller and Big Shot, and 54in (1.38m) to ride X-Scream and Insanity

If zooming up the tallest free-standing tower in the United States isn't exciting enough for you, the highest thrill rides in the world await you at the top, along with a revolving restaurant and breathtaking views.

On top of the world Marking the northern end of the Strip, the Stratosphere stands in the shadow of its 1,149ft (350m) tower, which is the main attraction. By means of speedy double-decker elevators, you can be at the 12-floor complex known as the pod, which sits at the 775ft (236m) level, in less than 30 seconds and enjoy the spectacular view, either from the indoor, climate-controlled observation lounge or the open-air deck. Beneath this is the revolving Top of the World gourmet restaurant (► 66).

High-level thrills, low-level fun The quest for superlative experiences and the ultimate in excitement led the owners of the Stratosphere to install attractions at the top of the tower that are definitely not for anyone who suffers from vertigo. High Roller loads within the pod on level 112, then hurtles around the tower on a track at speeds of up to 30mph (48kph), with some sharp angles. Big Shot, one level higher, propels passengers upward at 45mph (72kph), creating a G-force of four, then plummets at zero gravity. X-Scream dangles you off the side of the building, 100 levels up, while Insanity is the ultimate in thrill rides—you experience centrifugal forces of three Gs while being spun out 64ft (19m) beyond the edge of the Tower 900ft (274m) up. At the foot of the tower is the Strat-O-Fair, a 1960s-style midway (funfair). It has traditional games of skill, a carousel, a Ferris wheel and a toned-down version of Big Shot for kids—called Little Shot.

Downtown

Don't overlook this area, where it all began. With its old-world appeal, Downtown is where the spirit of Las Vegas' humble beginnings still lives on through original casino hotels like the Plaza, Golden Nugget and Golden Gate.

Origins Centered on Fremont Street between Main and 9th, the streets of Downtown are narrower, more low-key and less glamorous than the Strip. In the 1920s, Fremont Street was the first street in Las Vegas to be paved and have traffic lights, and by the 1930s it had the first licensed gaming hall. Downtown Las Vegas already had 36 years of history as the commercial heart of Vegas by the time the first casino resort, El Rancho, was built on the Strip in 1941.

Revitalization Downtown had lost much of its business to the Strip by the 1990s, when Vegas entrepreneur Steve Wynn and fellow hoteliers set about reinventing the area. They came up with the $70 million Fremont Street Experience (➤ 46), which succeeded in bringing in the punters once again and putting Glitter Gulch—as it is known -firmly back on the map.

More attractions A welcome addition in 2004 was the Neonopolis mall (➤ 73), where you can be dazzled by the signs at the Neon Museum (➤ 57). With its striking Victorian decor and genuine antiques, Main Street Station has one of the city's best casinos in terms of comfort and atmosphere, and it's smoke-free. The Arts Factory is a collecton of artists, architects, photographers and graphic designers exhibiting in galleries under one roof in the Gateway Arts District. You can experience more creative talent at First Friday, with live performances and other activities on the first Friday of each month.

HIGHLIGHTS

- Fremont Street Experience (➤ 46)
- Main Street Station
- Golden Nugget Casino (➤ 61)
- Neon Museum (➤ 57)
- The Arts Factory

INFORMATION

🔲 F2: Locator map C1
✉ Centered around Fremont and Main streets
🍴 Numerous
🚌 108, 301, 302
↔ Stratosphere Tower (➤ 44), Fremont Street Experience (➤ 46), Las Vegas Natural History Museum (➤ 47)

Fremont Street Experience

DID YOU KNOW?

- Fremont Street was the hub of Las Vegas for nearly four decades
- Each column supporting the overhead structure carries 400,000 lb (181,440kg) of weight
- The components for the light show produce 65,536 color combinations
- The show's sound system generates 540,000 watts

INFORMATION

www.vegasexperince.com
- F2: Locator map C1
- 425 Fremont Street
- 702/678-5777
- Every hour on the hour after dark
- 108, 301, 302
- Free
- Stratosphere Tower (➤ 44), Downtown (➤ 45), Las Vegas Natural History Museum (➤ 47)

Venture beyond the Strip and head north to the Downtown area after dark to see the only show of its kind in the world—a fantastic sound-and-light show on a massive frame that overarches a five-block area.

A high-tech marvel The specifications for the components of this display are impressive— 2 million light bulbs, 180 strobe lights, 64 variable-hued lighting installations that can produce a whole spectrum of shades, more than 30 moving, tilting mirrors that further increase the effect by reflecting the lights, and a state-of-the-art sound system that broadcasts concert-quality music through more than 200 speakers. The whole show is controlled by 126 computers, each with a capacity equal to 100 home PCs.

Under cover of lightness This glittering spectacular is based on a huge, solid frame that curves 90ft (27m) above traffic-free Fremont Street, between Main and 4th streets, covering an area of more than 4 acres (1.5ha). A number of the Downtown casinos, including the Golden Nugget, are within this area, adding to the overall effect with their illuminated facades. There are 16 massive columns and 43,000 struts supporting the frame, but once the show starts, you don't think about anything structural any more. It's a breathtaking experience that has been wowing the crowds here since 1995.

Fremont Street by day You might suppose that, by comparison, it's rather dull here during the day. But the display frame shelters a lively shopping mall, the sound system continues to pipe in music to shop by, and there are often free concerts and street performers to add to the festive mood.

Las Vegas Natural History Museum

This terrific museum is far from dull, and provides a welcome contrast to the high life and glitz of the shows and casinos. There are lots of interactive displays, live animals to pet, animatronic dinosaurs and much more.

Unique items When you consider all the museums in the cities of the United States, you might not expect a Las Vegas institution to have something the others don't. However, among the displays here are two particularly rare species—the African water chevrotain (a cross between a pig and a deer) and the Liberian zebra duiker. In addition, there are more than 26 species of stuffed animals mounted in cases, including the largest jaguar ever displayed and plenty of fish.

Marine world Opened in 2004, the Whales exhibit is part of the Marine Life Gallery and complements the shark displays featuring live leopard sharks and a shark egg hatchery. There is a scale model of an orca, also known as the killer whale, a melonhead whale and a beluga whale, complete with baby. You can learn about the behavior and conservation of these creatures. Don't miss the re-creation of the jaws of a 50ft-long (15m) prehistoric shark.

Fun with the animals This is by no means a dry and dusty museum full of stationary objects, though. Many of the displays are animated, including five robotic dinosaurs—the 35ft (10.5m) T-rex is very popular. There are also live animals on show that visitors are occasionally allowed to pet. The concept of the museum is to combine education with fun, and the popular interactive area is a great place for children to try out their skills as amateur archeologists and paleontologists.

HIGHLIGHTS

- Hands-on activity room
- Whales exhibition
- Marine Life Gallery
- Robotic T-rex and Dinosaur Gallery
- African Galleries

INFORMATION

www.lvnhm.org

🔲 G1: Locator map C1

✉ 900 Las Vegas Boulevard North

☎ 702/384-3466

🕐 Daily 9–4

🚌 113

💵 Inexpensive

↔ Downtown (➤ 45), Fremont Street Experience (➤ 46)

The museum's dinosaur display includes this lifelike triceratops

47

Red Rock Canyon

HIGHLIGHTS

- Scenic Loop
- Hiking trails—Ice Box Canyon, Pine Creek Canyon, Calico Tank
- Children's Discovery Trail
- Wild burros
- Wildlife, including mountain lions (rare and hard to spot)

INFORMATION

www.redrockcanyononly.org
- Off map at A2: Locator map Off A1
- South Nevada, 20 miles (32km) west of Las Vegas
- Red Rock Visitor Center: 702/515-5350
- Daily 6–5. Red Rock Visitor Center: daily 8–4.30
- Parking: inexpensive; free for hikers
- A choice of tours is available from Las Vegas (➤ 20). Don't feed any of the wildlife and be warned that the wild donkeys (burros) may bite or kick if you get too close. Take your own water—do not drink the water in the canyon

This canyon was created 65 million years ago when the Keystone Thrust Fault pushed one rock plate up over another. The resulting spectacular formations, in contrasting gray limestone and red sandstone, are awesome.

Focal point It's incredible to think that this striking canyon, set in the 197,000-acre (79,725ha) Red Rock Canyon National Conservation Area, is a mere 20-minute drive from the razzmatazz of Vegas. The focal point is the steep red rock escarpment more than 13 miles (21km) long and almost 3,000ft (915m) high. More canyons have been gouged out within the formation by constant snowmelt and rains, creating the present dramatic landscape.

Taking precautions The best place to start is at the Red Rock Visitor Center, which offers information and interpretation about all the recreational opportunities available, including hiking and climbing. It also has a recorded self-guide tour giving you a description of the geology and wildlife (all protected) in the area, and provides maps of hiking and bicycle trails and details of picnic sites. Park rangers are also on hand to give advice. It is essential to carry plenty of water if you are hiking, to take precautions against the fierce heat of the sun and to wear extra layers in winter. Climbing should be undertaken only by experts with the correct equipment. Stick to the trails and be aware of weather conditions—flash floods do occur.

Loop the loop For those staying in their cars, the 13-mile (21km) one-way Scenic Loop, leaving from the Visitor Center, gives the chance to see some of the best rock formations and to pause for photos at the Calico Vista viewpoints.

LAS VEGAS'
best

Shows

THE CIRQUE DU SOLEIL

This remarkable troupe, which originated in Montréal, has taken circus arts to unprecedented new levels with its breathtaking skills and supremely artistic concept shows. It has totally won over Las Vegas, with no less than four shows currently running. It's a good idea to make reservations because the shows sell out quickly.

Mystère is at Treasure Island (Wed–Tue 7.30 and 10.30pm Very expensive); **"O"** is at the Bellagio (Wed–Sun 7.30 and 10.30pm Very expensive); **Zumanity** is at New York–New York (Fri–Tue 7 and 10pm Very expensive); and **Kà** is at MGM Grand (Fri–Tue 7 and 10.30pm Very expensive).

There are rumors of a fifth production arriving at the Mirage during 2006, which will celebrate the musical legacy of the Beatles. For further information access www.cirquedusoleil.com

AN EVENING AT THE CAGE

This show elevated drag to an art form. The glittering cosmopolitan entertainment sees a cast of male impersonators transformed into unbelievably accurate representations of female superstars that might include Madonna, Cher or Diana Ross.
D5 Riviera, 2901 Las Vegas Boulevard South 702/794-9433 Wed–Mon 7.30pm 301, 302; Strip trolley Expensive

BLUE MAN GROUP

This has to be the most unusual show in Vegas—a group of guys with bright cobalt-blue bald heads, performing hilarious routines in which artistic canvases are created by the strangest means.
C7 The Venetian, 3355 Las Vegas Boulevard South 702/414-1000 Schedule varies 301, 302; Strip trolley Very expensive

CÉLINE DION: A NEW DAY...

Since taking up a three-year residency, this has become one of the biggest shows in Las Vegas, with a cast of dancers, musicians and aerialists supplementing the talents of Ms Dion. But there's much more to this production than her powerful voice. It is nothing short of a visual extravaganza, with action-packed sequences, and superb choreography and showmanship. When Céline Dion takes a vacation, Sir Elton John takes over. Sitting at his famous red grand piano he gives a flawless performance.
C7 Caesars Palace, 3570 Las Vegas Boulevard South 702/731-7110 Wed–Sun 8.30pm Flamingo/Caesars 301, 302; Strip trolley Very expensive

CLINT HOLMES: ALL ABOUT THE MUSIC

The multitalented Mr Holmes, the son of a jazz singer and opera singer, entertains with a mixture of velvety vocals, slick dance routines and comedy.
C7 Harrah's, 3475 Las Vegas Boulevard South 702/369-5000 Mon–Sat 7.30pm Harrah's/Imperial Palace 301, 302; Strip trolley Very expensive

DANNY GANS: THE MAN OF MANY VOICES

Impressionist extraordinare Danny Gans blends song, dance, comedy and acting into a seamless stream of up to 100 different characters a night.
C7 Mirage, 3400 Las Vegas Boulevard South 702/792-777 Tue–Thu, Sat, Sun 8pm 301, 302; Strip trolley Very expensive

DIRK ARTHUR: XTREME MAGIC

It's magic to the extreme, with revolutionary magician Dirk Arthur's fast-paced show interweaving dance, breathtaking magic and exotic animals.
C9 Tropicana, 3801 Las Vegas Boulevard South 702/739-

2411 or 800/829-9034 (box office) 🕐 Sat–Thu 2–4pm 🅿 MGM Grand 🚌 301, 302; Strip trolley 💵 Expensive

FOLIES BERGÈRE

With its roots in 19th-century Paris, the *Folies* has morphed into something that's pure American showbiz glitz. Beautiful dancing girls, variety acts, stunning (and revealing) costumes and sumptuous stage sets make this a spectacular and elaborate show.
➕ C9 ✉ Tropicana, 3801 Las Vegas Boulevard South ☎ 702/739-2411 🕐 Mon, Wed, Thu, Sun 7.30 and 10pm (topless), Tue, Fri 8.30pm (topless) 🅿 MGM Grand 🚌 301, 302; Strip trolley 💵 Expensive

JUBILEE!

Jubilee's scantily clad showgirls in massive headdresses and little else—many appear topless—remain as popular as when the show opened in 1981. Though the original concept remains unchanged, brand-new routines and segments are introduced on a regular basis, and no expense is spared.
➕ C7 ✉ Bally's, 3645 Las Vegas Boulevard South ☎ 702/739-4567 🕐 Sat–Thu 7.30 and 10.30pm 🅿 Bally's/Paris 🚌 301, 302; Strip trolley 💵 Expensive ❓ Minimum age limit 18 years

LANCE BURTON: MASTER MAGICIAN

A fascinating display of the illusionist's art, plus traditional sleight-of-hand tricks that leave the audiences gasping. A good family show.
➕ C8 ✉ Monte Carlo, 3770 Las Vegas Boulevard South ☎ 702/730-7160 🕐 Tue–Sat 7 and 10pm 🚌 301, 302; Strip trolley 💵 Very expensive

MAMA MIA!

Attracting rave reviews wherever in the world it is staged, this show combines the story of a mother and daughter, the daughter's three possible fathers, and a memorable wedding, with the music of Swedish supergroup ABBA. Reservations usually required.
➕ C9 ✉ Mandalay Bay, 3950 Las Vegas Boulevard South ☎ 702/632-7777 🕐 Mon–Thu 7pm, Sat, Sun 5 and 9pm 🚌 301, 302; Strip trolley 💵 Expensive

PENN AND TELLER

This talented partnership combines magic, illusions, juggling, comedy and stunts in an intelligent show.
➕ A7 ✉ Rio, 3700 West Flamingo Road ☎ 702/777-7777 🕐 Wed–Mon 9pm 🚌 202 💵 Very expensive

RON LUCAS

Clever artist Ron Lucas will have you believing his witty and somewhat weird puppets are real during his heady mix of stand-up comedy and ventriloquism.
➕ A7 ✉ Rio, 3700 West Flamingo Road ☎ 702/777-7777 🕐 Sat–Thu 3pm 🚌 202 💵 Expensive

A GOOD IMPRESSION

Most of the big singing stars wind up in Las Vegas at one time or another, and the city hates to see them go. And why should they, when there are some talented people out there who not only look the same, but also sound just like the real thing? There are currently two popular shows running that feature a string of superstar impersonators, presenting the music of Elvis, Madonna, Ricky Martin, the Blues Brothers, Gloria Estefan, the Temptations and others. **American Superstars** is at the Stratosphere (☎ 702/380-7777 🕐 Wed, Fri, Sat 7 and 10pm, Sun–Tue 7pm 💵 Expensive); **Legends in Concert** is at the Imperial Palace (☎ 702/731-3311 🕐 Mon–Sat 7.30 and 10.30pm 💵 Expensive).

53

Shows

COMING SOON

Headliners come and go in the city, some staying longer than others. But Las Vegas likes to keep its future big names under wraps, so you never know what's lined up. Recent superstars who have performed here include David Copperfield, U2, Paul McCartney and Barry Manilow.

New shows are opening all the time. One of the most recent is *Avenue Q*, set in a $40 million theater specially designed for the Broadway hit at the Wynn Vegas Hotel. Andrew Lloyd Webber's musical phenomenon *Phantom of the Opera* is due to open in spring 2006 in majestic grandeur at the Venetian.

As shows can close just like that, it is always best to check first before turning up– anyway, reservations are usually needed for the most popular ones.

A scene from the popular musical We Will Rock You

SIRENS OF TI

An exciting, swashbuckling battle between sexy sirens and renegade pirates that takes place at Siren's Cove, at the hotel entrance. There's music, seductive dancing and plenty of explosions.

🗓 C6 ✉ Treasure Island, 3300 Las Vegas Boulevard South ☎ 702/733-3111 🕐 Daily 6, 8 and 10pm (dependent on weather); shows last 90 mins 🚌 301, 302; Strip trolley 👆 Free

SPLASH

No longer an underwater ballet, this show continues to stun audiences with its world-class choreography, ice-skating sequences and other acts, such as the motorcycling Riders of the Thunderdome.

🗓 D5 ✉ Riviera, 2901 Las Vegas Boulevard South ☎ 702/734-9301 🕐 Tue–Sat 7 and 9.30pm 🚌 301, 302; Strip trolley 👆 Very expensive

STEVE WYRICK: MIND-BLOWING MAGIC

You won't believe your eyes when you witness illusions by this master of the art—including the "largest illusion in Las Vegas," in which a twin-engine airplane materializes out of nowhere.

🗓 C8 ✉ Aladdin, 3667 Las Vegas Boulevard South ☎ 702/785-5000 🕐 Wed–Mon 7 and 10pm 🚌 301, 302; Strip trolley 👆 Very expensive

VIVA LAS VEGAS

This is the longest-running afternoon show in Vegas, a traditional variety show with highly talented acts. There's singing, dancing, comedy and more.

🗓 E4 ✉ Stratosphere, 2000 Las Vegas Boulevard South ☎ 702/380-7777 🕐 Mon–Sat 2 and 4pm 🚌 301, 302 👆 Moderate

WAYNE NEWTON

Mr Las Vegas himself has been performing here since 1963. Newton's show is a Vegas institution and one of the city's biggest attractions. It's slick, exudes showmanship and is never the same two nights in a row. The show contains a variety of material that will include a medley of his best-loved ballads, with perhaps some blues numbers and even a few gospel songs thrown in for good measure.

🗓 D6 ✉ Stardust, 3000 Las Vegas Boulevard South ☎ 702/732-6325 🕐 Sat–Thu 9pm 🚌 301, 302; Strip trolley 👆 Expensive

WE WILL ROCK YOU

Fresh from London's West End to Las Vegas, this hit musical is a celebration of Queen's music, written by British comedian Ben Elton.

🗓 C8 ✉ Paris Las Vegas, 3655 Las Vegas Boulevard South ☎ 702/946-7000 🕐 Mon, Fri 9pm, Tue, Wed, Sat 7 and 10.30pm, Sun 5 and 9pm 🚉 Bally's/Paris 🚌 301, 302; Strip trolley 👆 Very expensive

Wedding Chapels

CHAPEL OF THE BELLS
Follow in the footsteps of Mickey Rooney, football legend Pelé and soldiers marrying before Desert Storm in this most polished of venues.
➕ E5 ✉ 2233 Las Vegas Boulevard South ☎ 702/735-6803
🚌 301, 302; Strip trolley

GRACELAND WEDDING CHAPEL AND THE VIVA LAS VEGAS WEDDING CHAPEL
Here, the congregation is gathered together in the sight of Elvis. The most renowned style of wedding in Las Vegas is, of course, the ceremony that's conducted by an Elvis look-alike. Both these chapels offer this to fans of the King.
➕ F3 ✉ 619 Las Vegas Boulevard South ☎ 702/474-6655
🚌 301, 302; Strip trolley
Viva Las Vegas Wedding Chapel
➕ E4 ✉ 1205 Las Vegas Boulevard South ☎ 702/384-0771
🚌 301, 302; Strip trolley

LITTLE CHURCH OF THE WEST
This wooden church, built in 1943, is all rustic charm and has hosted the weddings of Betty Grable, Zsa Zsa Gabor, Judy Garland and Dudley Moore. It's the perfect romantic backdrop.
➕ C10 ✉ 4617 Las Vegas Boulevard South ☎ 702/739-7971
🚌 301, 302; Strip trolley

LITTLE WHITE CHAPEL
The setting of many celebrity weddings (including one of Joan Collins' marriages), with traditional ceremonies around the clock—simply show up and wait your turn. The Little White Chapel in the Sky marries couples in a hot-air balloon.
➕ E4 ✉ 1301 Las Vegas Boulevard South ☎ 702/382-5943
🚌 301, 302; Strip trolley

SAN FRANCISCO SALLY'S VICTORIAN CHAPEL
This tiny wedding chapel offers an all-Victoriana experience. Rent the gear and play the part in an old-fashioned marriage extravaganza.
➕ E4 ✉ 1304 Las Vegas Boulevard South ☎ 702/385-7777
🚌 301, 302; Strip trolley

SPECIAL MEMORY CHAPEL
A more conventional New England-style wedding chapel with a romantic spiral staircase.
➕ G1 ✉ 800 South 4th Street ☎ 702/384-2211 🚌 301, 302

WEE KIRK O' THE HEATHER
Vegas' longest continually running chapel is renowned for a more simple yet elegant ceremony.
➕ Off map at G1 ✉ 231 Las Vegas Boulevard South ☎ 702/382-9830 🚌 301, 302; Strip trolley

TYING THE KNOT IN STYLE
Whether your ideal wedding is being married by Elvis, tying the knot in a hot-air balloon, going for the quick drive-through ceremony or just a traditional romantic approach, there's a chapel here that can oblige. Many hotels also have elegant wedding chapels, or you can opt for an outdoor location amid majestic Nevada mountains and canyons. Anything goes.

CANTERBURY WEDDING CHAPELS
With their cathedral-like vaulted ceilings, stained-glass windows and arched entrances, the Canterbury Wedding Chapels at the Excalibur (➤ 28) provide fairy-tale nuptials in ornate style. The bride and groom can even re-enact Arthurian legend and dress up in the costumes of King Arthur and Lady Guinevere.

The Little White Chapel even offers a 24-hour drive-through service

55

Museums

A CHANGE OF PACE

There's a suprising amount of serious culture in Las Vegas, and the surrounding area has some of the richest collections of art in the country. So when you grow weary of the glitz and glamor, take some time out to uncover the history of the city, its entrepreneurs' superb art collections and a bit more about Nevada, the Silver State.

Top: *Bellagio Gallery of Fine Art*
Above: *The Lied Discovery Children's Museum, a learning experience*

ATOMIC TESTING MUSEUM

Opened in February 2005, this is the first museum of its kind in the US and provides an interesting insight into the work of the Nevada Test Site and its impact. Three miles (5km) from the Strip, the museum is certainly something different and a long way from the superficial hype of Vegas. Interactive exhibits help you learn about the history of nuclear power.
➕ E7 ✉ 755 East Flamingo Road ☎ 702/794-5151 🕐 Mon–Sat 9–5, Sun 1–5 🚌 202 💵 Moderate

BELLAGIO GALLERY OF FINE ART

A welcome addition to the Bellagio (➤ 34), this was the first gallery on the Strip, showing a serious side to Las Vegas culture. The facility is a noncommercial venue showcasing two high-quality art exhibitions per year from major museums across the US and beyond.
➕ C7 ✉ Bellagio, 3600 Las Vegas Boulevard South ☎ 702/693-7111 🕐 Daily 9–9 🚌 301, 302; Strip trolley 💵 Moderate

ELVIS-A-RAMA

The world's largest collection of personal Elvis Presley items. Take the self-guiding tour to get all the latest details on the King, starting with an 80ft-long (24m) mural entitled *Elvis-A-Rama*. Almost $5 million worth of items include four of Presley's cars, his clothes, jewelry and other personal memorabilia.
➕ C6 ✉ 3401 South Industrial Road ☎ 702/309-7200 🕐 Daily 10–6 🚌 203 💵 Moderate

LAS VEGAS ART MUSEUM

Housed in a first-rate exhibition space attached to the Sahara West Library, this museum is dedicated to bringing quality art exhibitions to the community. The LVAM moved to its present premises in 1997 and is now affliated to the Smithsonian Museum.
➕ Off map at A5 ✉ 9600 West Sahara Avenue ☎ 702/360-8080 🕐 Tue–Sat 10–5, Sun 1–5 🚌 204 💵 Inexpensive

LIED DISCOVERY CHILDREN'S MUSEUM

This hands-on approach to learning is not just for children, as there is plenty to stimulate adults, too. Constantly changing exhibits introduce children to different careers from banking to mining. There are also exhibits of Las Vegas' most famous neon signs.
➕ F2 ✉ 833 Las Vegas Boulevard North ☎ 702/360-8080 🕐 Tue–Sat 10–5 🚌 113 💵 Inexpensive

LOST VEGAS GAMBLING MUSEUM

Discover the history of Vegas' casinos—see early photographs, learn about gaming personalities and influential mobsters, and check out memorabilia from gaming chips to slot machines. There are also displays on the Hoover Dam.

✚ F2 ✉ 450 Fremont Street, Downtown ☎ 702/385-1883
🕓 Daily 10–8 🚌 108, 301, 302 💷 Inexpensive

MARJORIE BARRICK MUSEUM OF NATURAL HISTORY

Less than 3 miles (5km) from the Strip on the university campus is this excellent museum devoted to the Native Americans of the region, the wildlife and also the history of ancient Mesoamerica.

✚ F8 ✉ 4505 South Maryland Parkway ☎ 702/895-3381
🕓 Mon–Fri 8–4.45, Sat 10–2 🚌 109 💷 Free

NEON MUSEUM

The Neon's mission is "to collect, preserve, study and exhibit neon signs and associated artifacts." This unusual museum is, in fact, an outdoor walking tour at the Fremont Street Experience in Downtown (►46). Objects date back to 1940 and are displayed as installation artworks. In addition, the museum has a neon sign "boneyard" on a Downtown site, where signs await restoration (groups of 10 or more can visit by appointment only on a fee-paying tour).

✚ F2 ✉ 3131 Las Vegas Boulevard South ☎ 702/387-NEON (6366) 🕓 Daily 24 hours 🚌 108, 301, 302 💷 Free

NEVADA STATE MUSEUM

It's a tranquil setting in Lorenzi Park, about 5 miles (8km) from the Strip, for the State Museum and Historical Society, dedicated to advancement of the knowledge of history and natural history of Nevada. On show there is life before Vegas, and you can view exhibits of dinosaurs and early man right through to the controversial nuclear testing program. Vegas is not forgotten, however, with photographic displays of its early years and neon signs.

✚ B2 ✉ 700 Twin Lakes Drive ☎ 702/486-5205 🕓 Daily 9–5
🚌 106, 208 💷 Inexpensive

THE WYNN COLLECTION OF FINE ART

Now housed in the Wynn Las Vegas resort hotel (►86), this is Steve Wynn's personal collection of artwork. Central is Pablo Picasso's *Le Rêve*, but more gems on view include works by Matisse, Rembrandt, Monet, Renoir, Gauguin, Van Gogh and Warhol. This is a collection to rival most.

✚ D6 ✉ Wynn Las Vegas, 3131 Las Vegas Boulevard South
☎ 702/770-3599 🕓 Tue–Sat 10–5, Sun 1–5 🚇 Las Vegas Convention Center 🚌 301, 302; Strip trolley 💷 Inexpensive

CLARK COUNTY HERITAGE MUSEUM

A little farther afield (20 miles/32km from the Strip), check out this interesting heritage museum (✚ Off map at H3 ✉ 1820 South Boulder Highway ☎ 702/455-7955 🕓 Daily 9–4.30 🚌 107 💷 Inexpensive). It takes you from prehistoric times, through mining and the coming of the railroad to the Strip we know today. Heritage Street is a re-created early city street, featuring seven restored historic houses, complete with period furniture. Other highlights include the 1931 Boulder City Train depot, a ghost town and a display of vintage cars. The remote location of the site also makes for a good photographic opportunity.

The lights are on at the Neon Museum

For Kids

ALL IN THE FAMILY

Don't run away with the idea that Las Vegas is a family destination. Beyond the thrill and simulator rides—many of which have height restrictions that rule out the very young—and the odd wildlife attraction, there is not a whole lot for kids to do. Not so long ago the city tried to broaden its appeal to children, and hotels such as the MGM Grand and Treasure Island began touting themselves as family properties. But visitors who had young children in tow didn't spend enough cash in the casinos, and thus had a negative impact on the economy. However, if you do choose to bring the kids, many hotels have daycare centers and children over the age of five can attend a lot of the shows (check the minimum age limits in advance).

The rock climbing wall at M&M's World Game Works

ETHEL M. CHOC FACTORY

Take a self-guiding audio tour to discover how Ethel Mars' huge chocolate enterprise began and get an insight into the production processes. At the end sample your favorite candy.

➕ Off map at H11 ✉ 2 Cactus Garden Drive, Henderson (8 miles/5km southeast of Las Vegas) ☎ 702/435-2641; www.ethelm.com 🕐 Daily 8.30–7 🚌 217 ✋ Free

GAMEWORKS

A creation from movie mogul Steven Spielberg that is the ultimate in interactive, virtual-reality arcade games; it is geared mostly toward teenagers.

➕ C8 ✉ Showcase Mall, 3785 Las Vegas Boulevard ☎ 702/432-4263; www.gameworks.com 🕐 Sun–Thu 10am–midnight, Fri, Sat 10am–1am (hours can vary) 🚇 MGM Grand 🚌 301, 302; Strip trolley ✋ Admission free; individual activities inexpensive

LAS VEGAS MINI GRAND PRIX

All sorts of carts for kids and adults, plus a dragon roller coaster, arcade games and other fun attractions.

➕ Off map at A1 ✉ 1401 North Rainbow Boulevard ☎ 702/259-7000 🕐 Sun–Thu 10–10, Fri, Sat 10am–11pm 🚌 101 ✋ Admission free; individual rides inexpensive ❓ Minimum height restriction of 36in (92cm) for the roller coaster

M&M'S WORLD

An interactive shopping and retail complex over four floors with thousands of M&M's brand merchandise items, plus a 3-D movie theater, an M&M's Racing Team store and a wall covered in a multitude of different colored plain and peanut M&Ms.

➕ C8 ✉ Showcase Mall, 3785 Las Vegas Boulevard ☎ 702/736-7611 🕐 Sun–Thu 9am–11pm, Fri, Sat 9am–midnight 🚇 MGM Grand 🚌 301, 302; Strip trolley ✋ Admission free; movie inexpensive

SCANDIA FAMILY FUN CENTER

Here are go-karts, batting cages, three 18-hole mini-golf courses, bumper boats and a video arcade.

➕ B6 ✉ 2900 Sirius Avenue ☎ 702/364-0070 🕐 Mar–Oct daily 24 hours; Nov–Feb Sun–Thu 10am–11pm, Fri, Sat 10am–midnight 🚌 106 ✋ Admission free; fee for activities; saver pass moderate

Viewpoints and Landmarks

EIFFEL TOWER
Paris Las Vegas (► 33) features an unmistakable landmark   a half-size Eiffel Tower. For one of the best views in town, take the glass elevator to the observation deck 100ft (30m) above the Strip.
✚ C8 ✉ Paris Las Vegas, 3655 Las Vegas Boulevard South ☎ 702/946-7000 ⏰ Daily 10am–1am (weather permitting) 💵 Moderate 🚇 Bally's/Paris 🚌 301, 302; Strip trolley

THE LION OUTSIDE MGM
Unlike its live counterparts inside the MGM Grand (► 30), this sedentary lion is made of bronze, is 45ft (14m) tall and weighs in at 100,000 lb (45,360kg). It represents MGM Studios' signature lion, Metro.
✚ C8 ✉ MGM Grand, 3799 Las Vegas Boulevard South 🚇 MGM Grand 🚌 301, 302; Strip trolley

PYRAMID AND SPHINX
A gigantic black-glass pyramid, complete with a massive 10-floor replica sphinx guarding its entrance, dominates the Luxor. With its high-intensity lights, the pyramid is actually visible from space.
✚ C9 ✉ Luxor, 3900 Las Vegas Boulevard South 🚌 301, 302; Strip trolley

ST. MARK'S SQUARE CAMPANILE
This replica of the campanile in Venice's St. Mark's Square towers 315ft (96m) over the Venetian resort.
✚ C7 ✉ The Venetian, 3355 Las Vegas Boulevard South ☎ 702/414-1000 🚌 301, 302; Strip trolley

STATUE OF LIBERTY
Standing in front of New York–New York (► 31), this well-known landmark is 150ft (46m) high and forms part of a re-creation of the Manhattan skyline.
✚ C8 ✉ New York–New York, 3790 Las Vegas Boulevard South ☎ 702/740-6969 🚇 MGM Grand 🚌 301, 302; Strip trolley

VEGAS VIC AND VEGAS VICKI
These famous neon signs are part of the Downtown after-dark scene; Vic is perched on top of the Pioneer Club and Vicki on the Girls of Glitter Gulch.
✚ F2 ✉ Downtown 🚌 108, 301, 302

WELCOME TO FABULOUS LAS VEGAS SIGN
This famous sign, designed in 1959, welcomes you as you enter Las Vegas at the south end of the Strip.
✚ C11 ✉ Las Vegas Boulevard South 🚌 301, 302

LAS VEGAS ARCHITECTURE

There was a time when Las Vegas had the monopoly on gambling in the US. Its hotels were large and luxurious enough, but there was nothing to match the fantastic architecture that distinguishes the city today. It all started when gambling was legalized in Atlantic City and Vegas needed something special to keep its edge on the market. That was when theme resorts began to change the face of the Strip. Later, when the city realized it was missing out on a huge section of the vacationing market, it started to develop spectacular resort hotels to bring in the nongambling public, too. For landmarks and spectacular views it would be hard to beat the Las Vegas skyline, which now includes many of the world's most famous architectural symbols.

The half-size Eiffel Tower at Paris Las Vegas stands 50 floors high

Spas

The spa at Bellagio has a typically opulent entrance

FOUR SEASONS HEALTH AND FITNESS CLUB

This is an exquisite facility for the ultimate pampering. Treatments include facials, body scrubs, massages and mud-treatments, and there are two private spa suites, with sauna, steam room, whirlpool tub and massage table. The fitness suite includes weights and cardiovascular equipment, saunas, steam rooms and Jacuzzis, and there's a jogging track through the beautiful grounds. Hotel guests only.

➕ C9 ✉ Four Seasons, 3950 Las Vegas Boulevard South ☎ 702/632-5302 🕐 Daily 6am–9pm 🚌 301, 302; Strip trolley

OASIS SPA

This is the only place in Vegas where you can have a relaxing massage or other treatment in the early hours after a night on the town. A whole range of exercise equipment—treadmills, bicycles, weight machines, climbing machines—is available here, along with such treatments as body wraps, body scrubs, massages, hydrotherapy and facials. There are tanning beds, too.

➕ C9 ✉ Luxor, 3900 Las Vegas Boulevard South ☎ 702/730-5724 🕐 Daily 24 hours 🚌 301, 302; Strip trolley

SPA AT BELLAGIO

You need to be a Bellagio guest to use the facility here, which includes Vichy showers (with 12 jets pounding you from all directions), massage, hydrotherapy and salt glows, plus exercise equipment and quality food at the juice bar.

➕ C7 ✉ Bellagio, 3600 Las Vegas Boulevard South ☎ 702/693-7472 🕐 Daily 6am–8pm 🚌 301, 302; Strip trolley

SPA AT CAESARS PALACE

In addition to the first-class spa treatments and exercise equipment here, there's a beautiful outdoor area, where you can relax amid statues and topiary beside three superb swimming pools. Luxury poolside cabanas are for rent, and come with wait service, TVs and massage service.

➕ C7 ✉ Caesars Palace, 3570 Las Vegas Boulevard South ☎ 702/731-7776 🕐 Daily 6am–8pm; hotel guests only on Fri and Sat 🚇 Flamingo/Caesars 🚌 301, 302; Strip trolley

SPA MANDALAY

This opulent facility has picture windows with a wonderful view over the hotel's lagoon and gardens. In addition to traditional treatments, there is a range of more exotic techniques, including ayurvedic relaxation and Swedish massage, while amenities include whirlpools with waterfalls, saunas and Swedish showers.

➕ C9 ✉ Mandalay Bay, 3950 Las Vegas Boulevard South ☎ 702/632-7220 🕐 Daily 6am–9pm 🚌 301, 302; Strip trolley

Casinos

BELLAGIO
The Bellagio casino oozes sophistication. Slot-machine carousels are encased in marble and wood, rather than the usual tasteless neon tubing, and custom-made carpets provide a stylish ambience.
➕ C7 ✉ 3600 Las Vegas Boulevard South ☎ 702/693-7111 🕐 Daily 24 hours 🚌 301, 302; Strip trolley

CAESARS PALACE
Cocktail waitresses in togas attend to your every need here under the watchful eye of marble Roman statues. High limits that can sometimes go through the roof make for an exciting atmosphere.
➕ C7 ✉ 3570 Las Vegas Boulevard South ☎ 702/731-7110 🕐 Daily 24 hours 🚉 Flamingo/Caesars 🚌 301, 302; Strip trolley

GOLDEN NUGGET
For a touch of nostalgia, come to one of the city's originals, opened in 1946. What this casino lacks in Vegas panache it more than makes up for in class.
➕ F2 ✉ 129 East Fremont Street ☎ 702/385-7111 🕐 Daily 24 hours 🚌 108, 301, 302

NEW YORK–NEW YORK
It's all rather impressive, with tuxedo-backed chairs setting the tone at this fun casino set against the backdrop of the Big Apple. Serious gamblers might find this larger-than-life casino a bit distracting, but there is one of the best selections of slot machines on the Strip.
➕ C8 ✉ 3790 Las Vegas Boulevard South ☎ 702/740 6969 🕐 Daily 24 hours 🚉 MGM Grand 🚌 301, 302; Strip trolley

RIO
It's carnival time every day at the Rio. Every hour on the hour from 4pm to 10pm, Mardi Gras floats suspended from the ceiling parade above the casino floor. In 2005, the Rio played host to the "World Series of Poker," the most famous and largest poker tournament in the world.
➕ A7 ✉ 3700 West Flamingo Road ☎ 702/777-7777 🕐 Daily 24 hours 🚌 202

THE VENETIAN
This replica of Venice's Doge's Palace is adorned with marble, chandeliers and opulent ceilings. High rollers at the tables are watched over by Tiepolo, Tintoretto and Titian paintings on the walls, while costumed opera singers compete with the clanging of slot machines. Slots include mega jackpot machines, and you can drive your jackpot home if you win one of the prestige cars that is up for grabs.
➕ C7 ✉ 3355 Las Vegas Boulevard South ☎ 702/414-1000 🕐 Daily 24 hours 🚌 301, 302; Strip trolley

TAKE A GAMBLE

Nevada law permits a wide variety of gaming, but the most popular flutters are roulette, blackjack, craps and slot machines. If you are new to the game, take some time to watch before actually taking the plunge; you could pick up a few tips from the hard-and-fast gamblers. Punters have to be 21 to play. Most casinos do not have windows or clocks, so you are unaware of time passing, and they will often keep you refuelled with free drinks and snacks. One benefit of all this cash changing hands is that most of the gaming taxes collected by the state are funneled into public education.

Roman statues oversee the gambling at Caesars Palace

The Great Outdoors

CITY PARKS

You don't have to go far to get away from the crowds in Las Vegas, as there are some green spaces right on the doorstep. Lorenzi Park, off Washington Avenue, just west of Downtown, is a great place for kids and those who like outdoor activities. Amenities include tennis, softball, an extensive playground, a huge 5-acre (2ha) pond, a rose garden, barbecue facilities and picnic tables. Sunset Park lies in the southeast of the city off Sunset Road and has such activities as archery, basketball, baseball, an exercise course, a playground, a jogging trail and a huge lake stocked with fish. Don't forget some bread to feed the ducks.

The alpine Mount Charleston region is great for hikers and horseback riders

CLARK COUNTY WETLANDS PARK

Just 8 miles (13km) east of the Strip, this environmentally conscious park has a visitor center where you can pick up trail maps. Bird-watching is popular, with recorded species including great blue herons, snowy egrets and black bellied whistling ducks.

➕ Off map at H9 ✉ 7050 Wetlands Park Lane ☎ 702/455-7522 🕐 Visitor center: daily 10–4. Nature center: daily dawn–dusk 🚌 202 then walk 1 mile (1.5km), or go by car ✋ Free

FLAMINGO WILDLIFE HABITAT

A lush 15-acre (6ha) paradise has been re-created at the Flamingo to provide a home to more than 300 exotic birds, including flamingos and penguins. There are also carp lagoons and leisure amenities.

➕ C7 ✉ Flamingo, 555 Las Vegas Boulevard South ☎ 702/733-3111 🕐 Daily 24 hours 🚇 Flamingo/Caesars 🚌 301, 302; Strip trolley ✋ Free

MOUNT CHARLESTON

Only 30 minutes' drive away and always cooler than Las Vegas—by as much as 40°F (22°C)—this lovely alpine wilderness is worth a visit. Together with the surrounding Toiyabe Forest, it is popular for hiking (52 miles/84km of trails), picnicking and camping. Nearby Lee Canyon is a great spot for skiing.

➕ Off map at A3 ✉ 35 miles (56km) northwest of Las Vegas 🚌 Organized tours or by car (check road conditions in winter) ✋ Free

SOUTHERN NEVADA ZOOLOGICAL-BOTANICAL PARK

Just beyond Texas Station, 6 miles (9.5km) northwest of Vegas, this small zoo is home to more than 200 species of plants and animals. Highlights are an Indo-Chinese tiger, Canadian otters, a couple of lions and a pair of fossas—an endangered species that forms the link between true cats and civets and the mongoose.

➕ B1 ✉ 1775 North Rancho ☎ 702/647-4685 🕐 Daily 9–5 🚌 106 ✋ Inexpensive

VALLEY OF FIRE STATE PARK

Nevada's first state park takes its name from its red sandstone rock formations. Formed millions of years ago by a shift in the earth's crust and eroded by water and wind, the resulting weird and wonderful shapes resemble everything from elephants to pianos. The visitor center provides trail maps and information.

➕ Off map at F1 ✉ 55 miles (88km) northeast of Las Vegas 🕐 Visitor center: daily 8.30–4.30 🚌 Organized tours or by car ✋ Parking inexpensive

LAS VEGAS
where to...

North American & Mexican

AUREOLE ($$$)

This restaurant has big windows, glass-covered waterfalls and a massive wine tower that waiters can be seen scaling in harnesses. Filet mignon with parsley custard is a stand-out on the first-class menu.

➕ C9 ✉ Mandalay Bay, 3950 Las Vegas Boulevard South ☎ 702/632-7401 🕐 Daily 6–11 🚍 301, 302; Strip trolley

BORDER GRILL ($$)

Come here for great Mexican home cooking in a lively setting. Lunch on spicy baby back ribs on the patio or get a take-out taco.

➕ C9 ✉ Mandalay Bay, 3950 Las Vegas Boulevard South ☎ 702/632-7403 🕐 Sun–Thu 11.30–10.30, Fri, Sat 11.30–11 🚍 301, 302; Strip trolley

DONA MARIA TAMALES ($)

Best here are the great tamales—shredded chicken, beef and pork wrapped in cornmeal.

➕ E3 ✉ 910 Las Vegas Boulevard South ☎ 702/382-6538 🕐 Daily 8am–10pm 🚍 301, 302

EMERIL'S NEW ORLEANS FISH HOUSE ($$$)

This is a re-creation of Emeril Lagasse's popular, sophisticated New Orleans restaurant. The menu includes barbecued shrimp, veal sirloin, garlic pork chop and sumptuous banana cream pie.

➕ C8 ✉ MGM Grand, 3799 Las Vegas Boulevard South ☎ 702/891-7374 🕐 Daily

11–2.30, 5.30–10.30 🚇 MGM Grand 🚍 301, 302; Strip trolley

HOUSE OF LORDS ($$)

Once the haunt of visiting stars, this comfortable restaurant remains popular for its traditional cuisine. Dishes include roasted crab cakes, prime rib and cherries jubilee.

➕ D5 ✉ Sahara, 2535 Las Vegas Boulevard South ☎ 702/737-2111 🕐 Daily 5–10 🚇 Sahara 🚍 301, 302; Strip trolley

POSTRIO ($$)

Enjoy Wolfgang Puck's American dishes in an elegant dining room or casual café on St. Mark's Square.

➕ C7 ✉ The Venetian, 3355 Las Vegas Boulevard South ☎ 702/796-1110 🕐 Sun–Thu 11.30–11, Fri, Sat 11.30am–midnight 🚍 301, 302; Strip trolley

SPAGO ($$$)

Pizzas, pastas, seafood, meat, poultry and homemade desserts get the Wolfgang Puck treatment.

➕ C7 ✉ Caesars Palace, 3570 Las Vegas Boulevard South ☎ 702/369-6300 🕐 Sun–Thu 6–10.30, Fri, Sat 5.30–11 🚇 Flamingo/Caesars 🚍 301, 302; Strip trolley

TOTO'S ($)

This family-run restaurant serves enormous helpings of good Mexican good. It's popular with locals who welcome the good value.

➕ H9 ✉ 2055 East Tropicana Avenue ☎ 702/895-7923 🕐 Sun–Thu 11–10, Fri, Sat 11–11

Italian

ANDIAMO ($$$)

Brightly lit, with lots of fresh flowers, this is a popular, fairly casual restaurant serving fine northern Italian cuisine.
🔢 E5 ⊠ Las Vegas Hilton, 3000 Paradise Road
☎ 702/732-5755 ⏲ Daily 5–11 🚌 Las Vegas Hilton
🚍 108

BATTISTA'S HOLE IN THE WALL ($$)

For more than 30 years people have been flocking here for the excellent Italian food, served with style.
🔢 C7 ⊠ 4041 Audrie Street
☎ 702/732-1424
⏲ Sun–Thu 5–10.30, Fri, Sat 5–11 🚌 Flamingo/Caesars
🚍 301, 302; Strip trolley

CANALETTO ($$$)

Where better to sample good northern Italian cuisine than on a re-creation of Venice's St. Mark's Square? Some little-known Italian wines are on offer, too.
🔢 C7 ⊠ The Venetian, 3377 Las Vegas Boulevard South
☎ 702/733-0070
⏲ Sun–Thu 11.30–11, Fri, Sat 11.30am–midnight 🚍 301, 302; Strip trolley

FIORE ($$$)

The superb, creatively presented food here includes pheasant ravioli and roasted rack of lamb. You can dine inside or on the patio.
🔢 A7 ⊠ Rio, 3700 West Flamingo Road ☎ 702/252-7777 ⏲ Daily 5–11 🚍 202

FRANCESCO'S ($$)

Superb fare—try the pancetta-wrapped scallops—is a real bonus at this friendly and relaxed restaurant.
🔢 C6 ⊠ Treasure Island, 3300 Las Vegas Boulevard South
☎ 702/894-7223 ⏲ Daily 5.30–10.30 🚍 301, 302; Strip trolley

RENOIR ($$$)

This is another artist-themed French restaurant (with real works of art). The gourmet cuisine is equally artistic.
🔢 C7 ⊠ Mirage, 3400 Las Vegas Boulevard South
☎ 702/791-7223 ⏲ Tue–Sat 5.30–9.30 🚍 301, 302; Strip trolley

STEFANO'S ($$)

Classy, but relaxed, this place serves up a wonderful *cioppino* (spicy tomato and seafood broth), *osso buco* and other northern Italian dishes, brought to the table by singing waiters.
🔢 F2 ⊠ Golden Nugget, 129 East Fremont Street
☎ 702/385-7111
⏲ Thu–Mon 5.30–10.30
🚍 108, 301, 302

STIVALI ($)

Large platters of pasta and excellent pizzas are dished up at this great family eatery.
🔢 D5 ⊠ Circus Circus, 2880 Las Vegas Boulevard South
☎ 702/691-5820 ⏲ Daily 5–10 🚍 301, 302; Strip trolley

VALENTINO ($$$)

Linger over superb modern Italian cuisine at this top-class restaurant.
🔢 C7 ⊠ The Venetian, 3355 Las Vegas Boulevard South
☎ 702/414-3000 ⏲ Daily 5.30–11 🚍 301, 302; Strip trolley

A NEW IMAGE

Until fairly recently, the only culinary experience for which Las Vegas was famous was the opportunity to stuff yourself with as much food as you could for a very reasonable price. Now it has become renowned for the amount of choice, with every kind of cuisine and style to suit every budget. For special-occasion dining in sumptuous surroundings, the best hotel restaurants are at the Bellagio, Mandalay Bay and the Venetian.

French & Other European

DINING ROOM WITH A VIEW

There are some wonderful spots in Vegas where you can savor great views while you eat, but here are two of the best. The Top of the World restaurant (▶ this page) is on the 106th floor of the Stratosphere Tower. It makes one revolution in 60 minutes, during which you can see the Strip, the mountains, the valleys and beyond. For a special night out, try the chic Eiffel Tower restaurant, located within the 50-floor replica at Paris Las Vegas (✉ 3655 Las Vegas Boulevard South ☎ 702/948-6937 ⏰ Daily 5.30–10.45). It serves the classic French cooking of chef J. Joho and offers great views of the Bellagio fountain show.

ANDRÉ'S ($$$)

This French restaurant is so good it has spawned a twin in Monte Carlo. There is a nice old-world atmosphere, romantic alcoves and food such as rib eye with pecan and Roquefort butter, plus decadent desserts.

✚ F3 ✉ 401 South 6th Street ☎ 702/385-5016 ⏰ Sun–Thu 5.30–9.30, Fri, Sat 5.30–10.30 🚃 108, 301, 302

CAFÉ HEIDELBERG ($)

A German restaurant serving traditional dishes such as goulash, schnitzels and stuffed cabbage rolls. There is also an on-site deli.

✚ E5 ✉ 604 East Sahara Avenue ☎ 702/731-5310 ⏰ Daily 11–10 🚃 204

DRAI'S ($$$)

Come here for excellent French food, a contemporary ambience and a divine chocolate mousse. Live jazz is played.

✚ C7 ✉ Barbary Coast, 3595 Las Vegas Boulevard South ☎ 702/737-7111 ⏰ Daily 5.30–midnight 🚃 301, 302; Strip trolley

ISIS ($$$)

Replica Egyptian treasures surround you as you dine here on such dishes as pheasant with *foie gras* and a version of baked Alaska.

✚ C9 ✉ Luxor, 3900 Las Vegas Boulevard South ☎ 702/262-4773 ⏰ Thu–Mon 5.30–11 🚃 301, 302; Strip trolley

MON AMI GABI ($$)

Enjoy fine French fare in the atrium here (with an open sunroof) or on the patio. Tables are set beneath sparkling white lights, from where you get a great view of the Bellagio's fountain show.

✚ C8 ✉ Paris Las Vegas, 3655 Las Vegas Boulevard South ☎ 702/944-GABI (4224) ⏰ Sun–Thu 11.30–1.30, 5–11, Fri, Sat 11.30–3.30, 5–midnight 🚃 Bally's/Paris 🚃 301, 302; Strip trolley

PICASSO ($$$)

This is among the best restaurants in Vegas, with refined cuisine reflecting places where the artist lived (south of France and Spain). And the Picasso paintings on the walls are authentic!

✚ C7 ✉ Bellagio, 3600 Las Vegas Boulevard South ☎ 702/693-7223 ⏰ Wed–Mon 6–9.30 🚃 301, 302; Strip trolley

RED SQUARE ($$)

Wash latkes and blinis down with vodka, or choose US and French dishes, in this Russian-themed restaurant.

✚ C9 ✉ Mandalay Bay, 3950 Las Vegas Boulevard South ☎ 702/632-7407 ⏰ Daily 5.30–midnight 🚃 301, 302; Strip trolley

TOP OF THE WORLD ($$$)

Enjoy delicious culinary creations in this revolving restaurant 833ft (254m) above the Strip. Unfortunately, however, the great view comes at sky-high prices.

✚ E4 ✉ Stratosphere Tower, 2000 Las Vegas Boulevard South ☎ 702/380-7711 ⏰ Sun–Thu 11–3, 5.30–10.30, Fri, Sat 11–3, 5.30–11 🚃 301, 302

Oriental

BENIHANA ($$)

Be entertained by the chefs at this Japanese *teppan* restaurant, as they prepare and cook the food in front of you.
E5 ⊠ Las Vegas Hilton, 3000 Paradise Road ☎ 702/732-5111 ① Daily 5–11 ⓖ Las Vegas Hilton 🚌 108

CHINA GRILL ($$$)

Come with a group of friends or family and prepare to splurge on the massive portions in this imaginative Asian restaurant. Food is cooked in woks or under the grill—fish may be served whole, including the head.
C9 ⊠ Mandalay Bay, 3950 Las Vegas Boulevard South ☎ 702/632-7404 ① Sun–Thu 5–11, Fri, Sat 5–midnight 🚌 301, 302; Strip trolley

HYAKUMI RESTAURANT AND SUSHI BAR ($$)

This is another Japanese restaurant where *teppan-yaki* chefs prepare your meal at your table with great flair and entertainment value. There's a good range of sake, too.
C7 ⊠ Caesars Palace, 3570 Las Vegas Boulevard South ☎ 702/731-7731 ① Daily 5–11 ⓖ Flamingo/Caesars 🚌 301, 302; Strip trolley

LILLIE LANGTRY'S ($$)

There's an odd mix of cultures at work here, but the cuisine is most definitely Chinese, and of exceptional quality. The Sichuan and Cantonese dishes include stir-fried lobster and Mongolian beef.
F2 ⊠ Golden Nugget, 129 East Fremont Street ☎ 702/385-7111 ① Daily 5–11 🚌 108, 301, 302

LOTUS OF SIAM ($)

The Lotus is one of only a few Thai restaurants in Las Vegas, and has a huge menu of tasty dishes such as *pad thai* and *mee krob*, plus daily specials. Let them know how hot you like your food and they'll prepare it accordingly. If you overdo it, have the coconut ice cream for dessert. Note the early closing time.
F5 ⊠ 953 East Sahara Avenue ☎ 702/735-3033 ① Daily 11.30–2, 5.30–9.30 🚌 204

NOBU ($$$)

This branch of the famous New York restaurant serves first-class sushi and exotic fish dishes. You'll be among a trendy crowd of diners.
E8 ⊠ Hard Rock, 4455 Paradise Road ☎ 702/693-5090 ① Mon–Sat 5–midnight 🚌 108, 213

NOODLE SHOP ($)

The food here really hits the spot when you need sustenance in the early hours—or at any time of the day or night, come to that. It offers more than 20 kinds of noodle and rice dishes, served hot and at lightning speed, plus barbecued meat dishes.
C9 ⊠ Mandalay Bay, 3950 Las Vegas Boulevard South ☎ 702/632-7777 ① Daily 24 hours 🚌 301, 302; Strip trolley

TASTE THE GOOD LIFE

In addition to the endless variety of eateries catering to visitors on a more restricted budget, a new type of restaurant has surfaced in Las Vegas. During the 1990s, fashionable eateries and stand-alone fine-dining establishments made their mark on the city. World-famous chefs with the best credentials—such as Puck, Lagasse, Palmer, Vongerichten, Mori, Sotelino and Matsuisa—were lured to Vegas to meet the demands of increasing numbers of sophisticated travelers visiting the city. As a result, food has evolved into another attraction with a Las Vegas flavor.

Steaks & Seafood

AJ'S STEAKHOUSE ($$$)

Masculine decor and trendy diners define this steak restaurant, but not as much as the food. Prime steaks and ribs, properly aged, are cooked to perfection.
➕ E8 ✉ Hard Rock, 4455 Paradise Road ☎ 702/693-5500 ⊙ Tue–Sat 6–11 🚌 108, 213

AQUA ($$$)

Constantly evolving and presenting the latest trends in cooking, this classy seafood restaurant offers tasty creations such as sea scallops with figs and lobster pot pie.
➕ C7 ✉ Bellagio, 3600 Las Vegas Boulevard South ☎ 702/693-7223 ⊙ Daily 5.30–10 🚌 301, 302; Strip trolley

AUSTEN'S STEAKHOUSE ($$)

It's worth the trip north of Downtown to this joint, which has gained a reputation for having the best prime beef in town.
➕ Off map at B1 ✉ Texas Station, 2101 Texas Star Lane ☎ 702/631-1000 ⊙ Sun–Thu 5–10, Fri, Sat 5–11 🚌 106

BINION'S RANCH STEAKHOUSE ($$$)

Succulent steaks and chops are served amid Victorian decor with spectacular views.
➕ F2 ✉ Binion's Horseshoe, 128 East Fremont Street ☎ 702/366-7304 ⊙ Daily 6–10.30 🚌 108, 301, 302

CHARLIE PARKER STEAK ($$$)

Subdued gleaming woodwork and bronze, and an exclusive atmosphere set the scene for a meal that might include charcoal-grilled filet mignon or steamed halibut.
➕ C9 ✉ Four Seasons, 3960 Las Vegas Boulevard South ☎ 702/632-5120 ⊙ Daily 5–10.30 🚌 301, 302; Strip trolley

KOKOMO'S ($$)

Tropical surroundings complement the delicious Hawaiian cuisine, including fish with broiled bananas and coconut shrimp.
➕ C7 ✉ Mirage, 3400 Las Vegas Boulevard South ☎ 702/791-7111 ⊙ Daily 5–10.30 🚌 301, 302; Strip trolley

KRISTOFER'S ($$)

The great steaks, tender ribs and broiled chicken in butter served here are matched by great prices; the barbecue sauce is wonderful, too.
➕ D5 ✉ Riviera, 2901 Las Vegas Boulevard South ☎ 702/794-9233 ⊙ Daily 5–10 🚌 301, 302; Strip trolley

LAWRY'S THE PRIME RIB ($$$)

Lawry's is popular for its pefectly cooked, tasty prime rib, which is carved at the table. Waitresses in stylish brown-and-white uniforms and starched white caps tend to your every need in the art deco surroundings, with big-band music playing in the background.
➕ D7 ✉ 4043 Howard Hughes Parkway ☎ 702/893-2223 ⊙ Sun–Thu 5–10, Fri, Sat 5–11 🚌 202

LIMERICKS ($$)

Comfy booths allow for peaceful dining in an atmosphere reminiscent of an English gentlemen's club. There are fine prime ribs and steaks, fresh seafood and lamb, and desserts made at the in-house bakery.

➕ F2 ✉ Fitzgeralds, 301 Fremont Street ☎ 702/388-2400 ⏰ Thu–Mon 5–11 🚌 108, 301, 302

NERO'S STEAK & SEAFOOD ($$$)

Maine lobster, swordfish and grilled *ahi* feature on the menu of this popular restaurant, along with hearty steaks.

➕ C7 ✉ Caesars Palace, 3750 Las Vegas Boulevard South ☎ 702/731-7110 ⏰ Daily 5–11 🚌 Flamingo/Caesars 🚌 301, 302; Strip trolley

NOBHILL ($$$)

A taste of San Francisco is brought to Vegas by celebrity chef Michael Mina. Finishing touches include five kinds of whipped potatoes to go with your tapioca-crusted rock cod, lobster pot pie or beef Wellington.

➕ C7 ✉ 3767 Las Vegas Boulevard South ☎ 702/891-7337 ⏰ Daily 5.30–11 🚌 301, 302; Strip trolley

SACRED SEA ROOM ($$$)

The murals of fishing Egyptians at this restaurant set the scene for its exotic seafood and meat dishes.

➕ C9 ✉ Luxor, 3900 Las Vegas Boulevard South ☎ 702/262-4772 ⏰ Thu–Mon 5–11 🚌 301, 302; Strip trolley

SAVANNA ($$)

There's an African theme here, and the menu has lots of variety, including steaks, pasta, jerk shrimp and oysters.

➕ C9 ✉ Tropicana, 3801 Las Vegas Boulevard South ☎ 702/739-2376 ⏰ Wed–Sat 5–11 🚇 MGM Grand 🚌 301, 302; Strip trolley

SMITH & WOLLENSKY STEAK HOUSE ($$$)

Big, energetic and informal, this great restaurant serves up some of the best steaks in Vegas, including a juicy Cajun rib eye and first-rate New York strip steak. Try the apple sauce with jalapeños.

➕ C8 ✉ 3767 Las Vegas Boulevard South ☎ 702/862-4100 ⏰ Restaurant: Mon–Fri noon–midnight, Sat, Sun 5pm–midnight. Grill: daily 11.30am–4am 🚌 301, 302; Strip trolley

THE STEAKHOUSE ($$)

This old-timer is popular for its succulent prime ribs and tasty grilled steaks, all at low prices. There's seafood, lobster, chicken and lamb as well.

➕ D5 ✉ Circus Circus, 2880 Las Vegas Boulevard South ☎ 702/734-0410 ⏰ Sun–Fri 5–10, Sat 5–11 🚌 301, 302; Strip trolley

ZAX ($$)

The chef's fusions of ethnic cuisines here create such dishes as chili seared scallops and Mojo New York steak.

➕ C9 ✉ Tropicana, 3801 Las Vegas Boulevard South ☎ 702/739-2376 ⏰ Wed–Sat 5–11 🚇 MGM Grand 🚌 301, 302; Strip trolley

DINNER SHOWS

If your time is short in Las Vegas you might like to take advantage of one of the dinner shows on offer, where you can eat and be thoroughly entertained at the same time. Probably the most popular of these is *Tournament of Kings* at the Excalibur (➤ 28). Also making headlines is *Tony 'n' Tina's Wedding* at the Rio (✉ 3700 West Flamingo Road ☎ 702/777-7777 ⏰ Daily 7pm), a wild-and-wacky show in which you are invited to join Tony and Tina for their wedding feast.

Cafés & Pub Grub

CHILD-FRIENDLY

Apart from the countless fast-food establishments selling hot dogs, burgers and pizzas, Las Vegas has many more options to prevent your kids from going hungry. Buffets enable them to pick and choose what they like, and most have an ice-cream machine that you can use to blackmail them into eating their greens. Themed restaurants that children will love include the Rainforest Café at the MGM Grand (⊠ 3799 Las Vegas Boulevard South ☎ 702/891-8580 ⑥ Sun–Thu 8am–11pm, Fri, Sat 8am–midnight), with jungle foliage, waterfalls, robotic animals and the occasional thunderstorm; the Hard Rock Café (⊠ 4475 Paradise Road at Harmon Avenue ☎ 702/733-8400 ⑥ Sun–Thu 11am–11.30pm, Fri, Sat 11am–1am), full to the brim with rock memorabilia; and the NASCAR Café (► 43), popular with sports fans.

CAFÉS

BINION'S COFFEE SHOP ($)

This is a great place for a light snack or something more substantial at a low price. The generous breakfasts are particularly good.
✛ F2 ⊠ Binion's Horseshoe, 128 Fremont Street ☎ 702/382-1600 ⑥ Daily 24 hours 🚌 108, 301, 302

EGG AND I ($)

Locals and visitors alike come here for the all-day (and most of the night) breakfast. The omelets and blueberry pancakes are particularly good choices.
✛ Off map at A5 ⊠ 4533 West Sahara Avenue ☎ 702/364-9686 ⑥ Daily 6am–3am 🚌 204

FOUR SEASONS HIGH TEA ($$)

It's quite a surprise to find that great British institution, the afternoon tea, in the middle of Las Vegas. There are dainty sandwiches, scones with cream and jam, and French pastries, plus a selection of fine teas. Piano music completes the elegant scene.
✛ C9 ⊠ Four Seasons, 3960 Las Vegas Boulevard South ☎ 702/632-5000 ⑥ Daily 2–5 🚌 301, 302; Strip trolley

HARLEY DAVIDSON CAFÉ ($)

Motorcycle buffs will enthuse over this American roadside café. Many gleaming machines are on display, including one owned by Elvis, and memorabilia covers the walls. Try the tollhouse-cookie pie.
✛ C7 ⊠ 3575 Las Vegas Boulevard South ☎ 702/740-4555 ⑥ Sun–Thu 11–11, Fri, Sat 11am–midnight 🚌 301, 302; Strip trolley

IL FORNAIO PANETTERIA ($)

It's worth making a special journey to this bakery café just for its espresso-mocha scone with chocolate chunks. There are also pastries, muffins and light meals.
✛ C8 ⊠ New York–New York, 3790 Las Vegas Boulevard South ☎ 702/740-6969 ⑥ Daily 7am–9pm 🚌 MGM Grand 🚌 301, 302; Strip trolley

PUB GRUB

MONTE CARLO PUB AND BREWERY ($)

Huge copper barrels enhance the rustic decor in this brewpub, where you can enjoy brick-oven pizzas, sandwiches, salads and platters…and, of course, the beer that is brewed on the premises.
✛ C8 ⊠ Monte Carlo, 3770 Las Vegas Boulevard South ☎ 702/730-7777 ⑥ Mon–Thu 11am–2am, Fri 11am–4am, Sat 10am–4am, Sun 10am–2am 🚌 301, 302; Strip trolley

TILTED KILT ($)

This Irish-American pub serves hearty Irish food, and Irish beer and stout are on tap. There's also Irish music and memorabilia, plus darts.
✛ A7 ⊠ Rio, 3700 West Flamingo Road ☎ 702/252-7777 ⑥ Daily 4pm–midnight 🚌 202

Buffets

BAY SIDE ($$)

Floor-to-ceiling windows here give sweeping views of the tropical lagoon outside. Although the buffet is not over-large, the cuisine is very good, with excellent salads, hearty meats and one of the better dessert selections, all made on the premises.

✚ C9 ⊠ Mandalay Bay, 3950 Las Vegas Boulevard South ☎ 702/632-7402 ⏰ Daily 7am–10pm 🚌 301, 302; Strip trolley

BELLAGIO BUFFET ($$)

More expensive than most buffets, this is probably the most highly regarded. It has many different types of cuisine, including Italian, Chinese and Japanese, in a European marketplace-style setting.

✚ C7 ⊠ Bellagio, 3600 Las Vegas Boulevard South ☎ 702/693-7111 ⏰ Sun–Thu 8am–10pm, Fri, Sat 8am–11pm 🚌 301, 302; Strip trolley

BIG KITCHEN ($)

Looking for all the world just like a gigantic kitchen, this buffet offers excellent value and hardly any waiting time. An enormous selection of such comfort foods as fried chicken and meat loaf sits alongside more interesting seafood and Chinese specialties, and the portions are big.

✚ C7 ⊠ Bally's, 3645 Las Vegas Boulevard South ☎ 702/739-4111 ⏰ Daily 7–2, 4–10 🚇 Bally's/Paris 🚌 301, 302; Strip trolley

CARNIVAL WORLD ($)

This is one of the best buffets in Las Vegas, with chefs cooking on view at various points around the serving islands. There are 11 styles of cuisine, from Brazilian to Mongolian.

✚ A7 ⊠ Rio, 3700 West Flamingo Road ☎ 702/252-7777 ⏰ Daily 7.30am–10pm 🚌 202

GARDEN COURT ($)

Watch your food being prepared at what is said to be Downtown's best buffet. On the nine counters are American, Pacific Rim, Chinese and Mexican dishes.

✚ F2 ⊠ Main Street Station, 200 North Main Street ☎ 702/387-1896 ⏰ Daily 7–10.30, 11–3, 4–10 🚌 108, 301, 302

PARADISE GARDEN ($)

Enjoy the view of cascading waterfalls and wildlife through large picture windows while you dine on crab, shrimp, prime rib, large salads and everything else in between. There's also a large dessert choice.

✚ C7 ⊠ Flamingo, 3555 Las Vegas Boulevard ☎ 702/733-3111 ⏰ Daily 7–2.30, 4.30–10 🚇 Flamingo/Caesars 🚌 301, 302; Strip trolley

VILLAGE SEAFOOD ($$)

Fish, fish and more fish—in fact, nothing but seafood is served here. Even so, there's plenty of choice, with dishes prepared in just about every way you could imagine.

✚ A7 ⊠ Rio, 3700 West Flamingo Road ☎ 702/252-7777 ⏰ Daily 4–10 🚌 202

BUFFET KNOW-HOW

Buffets offer breakfast, lunch and dinner, with a different range of food available at each meal. They are a great option for families, particularly those that include fussy eaters, because there is sure to be something for everyone. Buffets also offer tremendous value for money. This does, of course, mean that they are popular and lines can be long, especially at peak times—at the most popular buffets, it can take up to three hours to eat your meal.

Shopping Malls

OPENING HOURS

The larger malls and arcades are generally open Monday to Saturday 10–9, with shorter hours on Sunday. Some of the shops at larger hotel malls, such as Caesars Palace, may stay open until 11pm. Smaller independent and nonchain stores may shut at 6pm and don't open on Sunday.

HOTEL SHOPPING

You will find many familiar stores in hotel malls, such as Gap, Victoria's Secret, Tommy Bahama and Levi's Original, and the classier places will have designer boutiques like Prada and Hermès, too. You won't find the big department stores here, but you'll be able to buy a good range of items, including more mundane requirements such as toiletries, cosmetics and magazines. Souvenirs may include pieces that reflect the hotel's theme, or merchandise from the permanent shows and visiting entertainers.

HOTEL MALLS

DESERT PASSAGE (➤ 32)

THE FORUM (➤ 35)

GIZA GALLERIA

The Egyptian-theme shopping here includes both genuine and reproduction antiques, as well as kids' clothing and toys and a cosmetics store.

➕ C9 ✉ Luxor, 3900 Las Vegas Boulevard South ☎ 702/262-4000 🚌 301, 302; Strip trolley

GRAND CANAL SHOPPES

This chic, Italian-themed mall stretches along a replica of Venice's Grand Canal. Here you'll find 75 of the most exclusive stores in the world.

➕ C7 ✉ The Venetian, 3355 Las Vegas Boulevard South ☎ 702/414-4500 🚌 301, 302; Strip trolley

MANDALAY PLACE

A sky bridge connecting Mandalay Bay with the Luxor is home to a number of superior retailers. These include a good cigar shop, a swimwear boutique, a shop selling hand-carved Balinese furniture and an excellent florist.

➕ C9 ✉ Mandalay Bay, 3930 Las Vegas Boulevard South ☎ 702/632-9325 🚌 301, 302; Strip trolley

MASQUERADE VILLAGE

Stroll down the tiled streets here to find quirky places such as the Nawlins Store, carrying voodoo supplies and good luck charms. Elsewhere in the mall, sportswear and memorabilia are on sale.

➕ A7 ✉ Rio, 3700 West Flamingo Road ☎ 702/777-7777 🚌 202

MEDIEVAL VILLAGE

Well and truly carrying on the medieval theme, this mall includes Merlin's Mystic Shoppe, selling magic tricks and accoutrements, a medieval hatter, and a place where you can buy replica swords and shields (and the occasional suit of armor).

➕ C9 ✉ Excalibur, 3850 Las Vegas Boulevard South ☎ 702/597-7777 🚌 301, 302; Strip trolley

STREET OF DREAMS

A modest mall with clothing boutiques, plus the fascinating Lance Burton Magic Shop, with souvenirs and magic tricks to remind you of the master illusionist's show (➤ 53).

➕ C8 ✉ Monte Carlo, 3770 Las Vegas Boulevard South ☎ 702/730-7777 🚌 301, 302; Strip trolley

VIA BELLAGIO

This opulent mall will tempt you with its exquisite fashion and jewelry collections from world-renowned designers Giorgio Armani, Chanel, Gucci, Prada, Tiffany & Co. and lots more.

➕ C7 ✉ Bellagio, 3600 Las Vegas Boulevard South ☎ 702/693-7111 🚌 301, 302; Strip trolley

WYNN ESPLANADE
The endless list of exclusive names can't fail to impress at this new luxury hotel mall. The first Jean Paul Gaultier store in the US opened here and there is even a Ferrari and Maserati showroom.
➕ D6 ✉ Wynn Las Vegas, 3131 Las Vegas Boulevard South ☎ 702/770-7000 ⊙ Las Vegas Convention Center 🚌 301, 302; Strip trolley

OTHER MALLS

BOULEVARD MALL
Although this is the biggest shopping mall in Las Vegas, it is relatively tranquil, with a lovely landscaped atrium. Anchors include Sears, Macy's and JCPenney, and you'll find all the major chain stores.
➕ F6 ✉ 3528 South Maryland Parkway ☎ 702/732-9197 🚌 109

CHINATOWN PLAZA
More than 25 vendors can be found in this red-roof Asian shopping mall, selling ceramics, clothing and handmade furniture.
➕ Off map at A6 ✉ 4215 Spring Mountain Road ☎ 702/221-8448 🚌 203

FASHION SHOW MALL
This classy mall is among the 10 largest in the US. Quality stores include Saks Fifth Avenue, Nordstrom, Macy's, Neiman Marcus and Bloomingdale's, and there are lots of eateries.
➕ C6 ✉ 3200 Las Vegas Boulevard South ☎ 702/369-0704 🚌 301, 302; Strip trolley

GALLERIA AT SUNSET
Nine miles (16km) southeast of Downtown are the 140-plus shops of this mall, selling everything from clothing and shoes to electronics and home furnishings. Its anchors are JCPenney, Dillard's, Mervyn's California and Robinsons-May.
➕ Off map at H11 ✉ 1300 West Sunset Boulevard, Henderson ☎ 702/434-0202 🚌 212

HAWAIIAN MARKETPLACE
Inspired by the famous International Market Place in Waikiki, this Hawaiian-theme mall is in a wonderful setting of Polynesian flora and tiki statues. Pacific dance performers entertain you as you peruse the interesting stores.
➕ C8 ✉ 3743 Las Vegas Boulevard South ☎ 702/795-2247 🚌 301, 302; Strip trolley

THE MEADOWS
This is yet another huge mall, made up of more than 140 main-street names and department stores such as Macy's, Sears and JCPenney.
➕ A2 ✉ 4300 Meadows Lane (at intersection of Valley View and US95) ☎ 702/878-3331 🚌 103, 104

NEONOPOLIS
In addition to the usual shops and restaurants, this three-level mall has a multiplex cinema (see panel ► 81) and entertainment complex.
➕ F2 ✉ 450 Fremont Street ☎ 702/477-0470 🚌 108, 301, 302

HUNTING OUT BARGAINS
Downtown malls will sometimes have better prices than the same stores in the hotel shopping malls—and they are also less crowded. But for real bargains, head to the outlet malls. These carry discounted end-of-line, out-of-season and surplus stock, and include familiar chain stores and shops selling designer fashions, homewares and sporting goods. Just make sure you are getting top-quality items and not seconds or damaged goods. Some outlet malls have a shuttle service from hotels on the Strip. Try Belz Factory Outlet World (✉ 7400 Las Vegas Boulevard South ☎ 702/896-5599), Fashion Outlet of Las Vegas (✉ 32100 Las Vegas Boulevard South ☎ 702/874-1400) or Primm (✉ About 35 miles/55km south of Vegas, near the Nevada–California state line).

Shoes & Accessories

ALL THAT SPARKLES

In a city where more than a thousand weddings take place every year, it comes as no surprise that there is a great demand for fine jewelry stores in Las Vegas. And, needless to say, wedding rings are one of the top-selling items. At the Bellagio is the prestigious jeweler Fred Leighton (✉ 3600 Las Vegas Boulevard South ☎ 702/693-7050), who has been in the business for more than 25 years. His collection of rare and collectible jewels has made him the first port of call for many celebrities—the likes of Sharon Stone, Madonna and Cameron Diaz have been loaned his pieces to wear to the Oscars.

ARTEFFECTS

The innovative shoes and accessories here are made in wonderful fabrics and leathers, and are at the cutting edge of fashion.

➕ C6 ✉ Fashion Show Mall, 3200 Las Vegas Boulevard South ☎ 702/796-7463 🚍 301, 302; Strip trolley

COWTOWN BOOTS

Great Western clothing and cowboy boots are sold here, mostly at a good discount. It's the largest outlet of its kind in Nevada.

➕ E5 ✉ 2989 South Paradise Road ☎ 702/737-8469 🚍 108

JACQUELINE JARROT

Come here for trendy high-end accessories in the latest designs— handbags, costume jewelry, shoes, belts— from more than 300 designers. The shop is popular with celebrities.

➕ C8 ✉ Desert Passage, 3667 Las Vegas Boulevard South ☎ 702/731-3200 🚇 Bally's/Paris 🚍 301, 302; Strip trolley

JANA'S JADE GALLERY

This gallery sells an unusual and fascinating selection of hand-crafted jade jewelry.

➕ Off map at A6 ✉ Chinatown Plaza, 4215 Spring Mountain Road ☎ 702/227-9198 🚍 203

PEARL MOON BOUTIQUE

It's a bit on the pricey side, but the selection of swimwear, hats, sunglasses and sandals here is better quality than you'll find at other shops on the Strip.

➕ C9 ✉ Mandalay Bay, 3950 Las Vegas Bolevard South ☎ 702/632-9325 🚍 301, 302; Strip trolley

PROMENADE FOOTWEAR

The men's and women's designer shoes here are from such famous names as Diesel, Bunker and Kenneth Cole New York.

➕ C8 ✉ Desert Passage, 3667 Las Vegas Boulevard South ☎ 702/796-7463 🚇 Bally's/Paris 🚍 301, 302; Strip trolley

SERGE'S SHOWGIRL WIGS

What better way to top off an outfit than by pulling on a superstar's hairdo (or even a regular style)? This store has around 10,000 wigs, of all shapes, sizes and shades, and you can even top one with a showgirl headdress.

➕ F5 ✉ Commercial Center Plaza, 953 East Sahara Avenue ☎ 702/732-1015 🚍 204

STILETTO

The diverse range of fashion shoes at Stiletto includes footwear by Charles David, Natalie M, Via Spiga and Donald Pliner.

➕ C6 ✉ Fashion Show Mall, 3200 Las Vegas Boulevard South ☎ 702/791-0505 🚍 301, 302; Strip trolley

TOWER OF JEWELS

The exquisite jewelry sold here is custom-made by skilled craftsmen.

➕ E5 ✉ 896 East Sahara Avenue ☎ 702/735-4145 🚍 204

Antiques & Collectibles

ANTIQUES AT THE MARKET

A small warehouse of 60-plus dealers, this new addition for antiques lovers is near the airport. It's a great place for unusual finds.

✚ H11 ✉ 6665 South Eastern Avenue ☎ 702/307-3960 🚌 110

THE ATTIC

Feel like you're a child again rummaging through grandma's attic at this fascinating place. There is a hidden treasure in every corner, including retro and vintage clothing, collectibles, furniture, jewelry, old radios, TVs, cameras and appliances.

✚ E3 ✉ 1018 South Main Street ☎ 702/388-4088 🚌 108

FIELD OF DREAMS

This is the place for one-offs of sport and celebrity memorabilia, from items such as an electric guitar signed by musician Carlos Santana to a jersey autographed by football player Dan Marino.

✚ B7 ✉ Masquerade Village, Rio, 3700 West Flamingo Road ☎ 702/221-9144 🚌 202

FUNK HOUSE

One of the best antiques stores in the city is the creation of Cindy Funkhouser. Her growing collection includes late-1950s and early-1960s furniture, glass, jewelry, rugs, paintings and toys.

✚ E3 ✉ 1228 South Casino Center Boulevard ☎ 702/678-6278 🚌 108

RED ROOSTER ANTIQUES MALL

Housed in a former bottling plant, this labyrinth of rooms conceals stands cluttered with postcards, casino memorabilia, 1950s furniture and more.

✚ D3 ✉ 1109 Western Avenue ☎ 702/382-5253 🚌 301, 302; Strip trolley

SAMPLER SHOPPES

In this mall-like setup some 200 small antiques dealers sell all sorts of goods under one roof, from clothing to silver, furniture and toys.

✚ Off map at A8 ✉ 6115 West Tropicana Avenue ☎ 702/368-1170 🚌 201

SHOWCASE SLOTS & ANTIQUES

This is a nostalgic collection of antique slot machines, early video poker machines, jukeboxes and neon signs.

✚ B7 ✉ 4305 South Industrial Road ☎ 702/740-5722 🚌 203

SILVER HORSE ANTIQUES

Lamps, furniture, glass and collectibles are just a few of the items hidden here.

✚ H3 ✉ 1651 East Charleston Boulevard ☎ 702/385-2700 🚌 206

TOYS OF YESTERYEAR

This tiny little place will take you back a few years with its wonderful collection of lovely old trains sets, windup toys, dolls and books.

✚ H3 ✉ 2028 East Charleston Boulevard ☎ 702/598-4030 🚌 206

ANTIQUES TRAIL

Believe it or not, Las Vegas has accumulated quite a few antiques stores over the years, most of them in the Downtown area around the east end of Charleston Boulevard. Here, knowledgeable antiques dealers have set up shop in tiny 1930s converted houses lining both sides of the street. If you stop off first at Silver Horse Antiques (▶ this page), you can collect a map that shows you where all the other shops are located and lists their opening hours.

Fashion

VINTAGE CLOTHING

The resurging popularity of retro styles in Las Vegas has led to an increase in the number of vintage and secondhand stores selling authentic 1960s and 1970s clothes. Retro Vintage Couture (⊠ 906 South Valley Drive ☎ 702/877-8989) stocks real retro fashions from such design houses as Gucci and Chanel. The Attic (► 75) also has a wonderful selection of retro and vintage clothing.

BEBE

This sassy boutique sells sleek tailored designs and curve-hugging wear inspired by the latest trends. There are branches at Desert Passage and The Forum.
✚ C6 ⊠ Fashion Show Mall, 3200 Las Vegas Boulevard South ☎ 702/892-8083 🚌 301, 302; Strip trolley

BETSEY JOHNSON

Flowing fabrics with beaded and embroidered detail are the style at this wacky shop for a wacky clientele. There's another branch at Desert Passage.
✚ C6 ⊠ Fashion Show Mall, 3200 Las Vegas Boulevard South ☎ 702/735-3338 🚌 301, 302; Strip trolley

CAROLINA HERRERA

Opened in 2004, this store is dedicated to Herrera's lifestyle collection for men and women. The range includes chic tailored suits, glam evening wear, cotton shirts and accessories.
✚ C7 ⊠ The Forum, 3500 Las Vegas Boulevard South ☎ 702/733-9000 🚌 301, 302; Strip trolley

GIANNI VERSACE

The late designer's colorful Italian style is obvious in the garments sold here, all made from the finest fabrics. The company's signature lion's head appears on everything. Another branch is at the Bellagio.
✚ C7 ⊠ The Forum, 3500 Las Vegas Boulevard South ☎ 702/796-7222 🚌 301, 302; Strip trolley

JEAN PAUL GAULTIER

When the Wynn Las Vegas hotel opened in 2005, it was the ideal spot for Gaultier's first venture in the US. The shop sells clothing for men and women in Jean Paul's distinct style, as well as the designer's famous fragrances.
✚ D6 ⊠ Wynn Las Vegas, 3131 Las Vegas Boulevard South ☎ 702/770-7800 🚇 Las Vegas Convention Center 🚌 301, 302; Strip trolley

TALULAH G

Come here to see what's in vogue for the young and trendy. Designs by Marc Jacobs, Vanessa Bruno, Jiwon Park and Stella McCartney attract celebrity shoppers.
✚ C6 ⊠ Fashion Show Mall, 3200 Las Vegas Boulevard South ☎ 702/737-6000 🚌 301, 302; Strip trolley

VILLA MODA

Elegant men's and women's clothing from European designers, including Versace, is sold here. You can buy shirts, jeans and jackets made from Spanish leather.
✚ C6 ⊠ Fashion Show Mall, 3200 Las Vegas Boulevard South ☎ 702/733-6776 🚌 301, 302; Strip trolley

WHITE HOUSE/BLACK MARKET

The striking black-and-white clothes and accessories here are aimed at the confident young woman. Another branch is at Desert Passage.
✚ C6 ⊠ Fashion Show Mall, 3200 Las Vegas Boulevard South ☎ 702/697-0247 🚌 301, 302; Strip trolley

Crafts & Souvenirs

BONANZA GIFT STORE

The self-styled "largest souvenir store in the world" has a mind-boggling array of tacky mementos, T-shirts and postcards. It's worth a visit, just to see how tasteless it can all get.
➕ D5 ✉ 2460 Las Vegas Boulevard South ☎ 702/384-0005 🚌 301, 302; Strip trolley

CHIHULY STORE

This shop has a good representation of the respected glass sculptor's vibrant hand-blown pieces. It's fitting that Chihuly opened his first gallery here—his biggest sculpture hangs from the Bellagio lobby's ceiling (➤ 34).
➕ C7 ✉ Bellagio, 3600 Las Vegas Boulevard South ☎ 702/693-7995 🚌 301, 302; Strip trolley

DRAGON'S LAIR

This is the place for full-size replicas of swords, shields and the odd suit of armor. More portable souvenirs include crystals, dragon sculptures and Merlin figurines.
➕ C9 ✉ Excalibur, 3850 Las Vegas Boulevard South ☎ 702/597-7777 🚌 301, 302; Strip trolley

GAMBLER'S GENERAL STORE

What better souvenir of a trip to Las Vegas than something with a gambling theme? Amaze your friends with a roulette wheel, blackjack table or slot machine. The used-card decks and gambling chips from major casinos are good, inexpensive buys.
➕ E3 ✉ 800 South Main Street ☎ 702/382-9903 🚌 108

LAS VEGAS INDIAN CENTER

This store has a great selection of Native American crafts, clothing, artworks, music and books.
➕ C2 ✉ 2300 West Bonanza Boulevard ☎ 702/647-5842 🚌 215

MIKIMOTO

Exquisite Akoya cultured pearls and South Sea pearl jewelry are sold here among other gift items.
➕ C7 ✉ Grand Canal Shoppes, 3355 Las Vegas Boulevard South ☎ 702/414-3900 🚌 301, 302; Strip trolley

RON LEE'S WORLD OF CLOWNS

This large gallery pays homage to the artist's stunning work. It displays the largest line of limited-edition clown figurine sculptures in the world.
➕ C8 ✉ Desert Passage, 3667 Las Vegas Boulevard South ☎ 702/866-0710 🚇 Bally's/Paris 🚌 301, 302; Strip trolley

WORLD OF COCA-COLA STORE

Much more than just a store, this is a living-history museum dedicated to the famous soda. Every conceivable Coca-Cola merchandise is for sale, and a huge coke bottle will transport you to the three levels.
➕ C8 ✉ Showcase Mall, 3785 Las Vegas Boulevard South ☎ 702/597-3122 🚇 MGM Grand 🚌 301, 302; Strip trolley

JUST FOR FUN

There's no doubt about it, Las Vegas is chock-full of enough tacky souvenirs to be able to supply the rest of the world's major tourist spots. But this is Vegas after all, and kitsch is just another facet of its fun character. Top of the most-wanted list of enviable souvenirs are jigsaw puzzles of the Strip, personalized poker chips, Elvis sunglasses with fake sideburns, dice-decorated clocks and other gambling mementos. One sure bet you can put your money on in Vegas is that not many people will leave without at least one item packed in their suitcase that announces to the world they have visited Sin City.

Food & Wine

GREEK FOOD FESTIVAL

What was once a one-day event has now grown into a four-day extravaganza. This annual festival takes place at St. John the Baptist Orthodox Church (✉ 5300 El Camino Road ☎ 702/221-8245) toward the end of September, and showcases an array of Greek food and culture. If you enjoy Greek cuisine it is a great opportunity to sample such delights as *saganaki* (fried cheese) and *tzatziki* (cucumber and yogurt dip) outdoors with *bouzoukis* playing and costumed folk dancers entertaining.

FREEDS BAKERY

This very successful family business has been producing the finest baked goods in the Las Vegas area for more than 44 years. Check out their specialty cookies and cakes, and the exquisite wedding cakes.
✚ H9 ✉ 4780 South Eastern Avenue ☎ 702/456-7762 🖥 110

KRISPY KREME DOUGHNUTS

The doughnuts here are based on a secret recipe that was obtained from a French chef in 1937. Indulge in the original glazed doughnuts or try one of the many other varieties. There are several branches throughout the city.
✚ C9 ✉ Excalibur, 3850 Las Vegas Boulevard South ☎ 702/736-5235 🖥 301, 302; Strip trolley

M&M'S WORLD

A tourist attraction as well as a candy store, this place has a huge selection of well-known confectionery brands, including a vast array of liqueur-filled chocolates and, of course, M&M's.
✚ C8 ✉ Showcase Mall, 3785 Las Vegas Boulevard South ☎ 702/736-7611 🖥 301, 302; Strip trolley

MERCADO BUENOS AIRES

If you have a hankering for South American delicacies, head for this authentic Argentinian market and deli.
✚ B6 ✉ 5300 West Spring Mountain Road ☎ 702/257-3331 🖥 203

SIENA DELI

For a taste of Italy, visit this tiny deli selling authentic Italian goods: homemade pastas, imported cheeses, olive oils. You can stop for a quick snack to try the quality produce.
✚ H9 ✉ Suite 22, Renaissance Plaza, 2250 East Tropicana Avenue ☎ 702/736-8424 🖥 201

TEUSCHER

Swiss chocolate-maker Dolf Teuscher uses only the very best ingredients in his freshly prepared luscious chocolates.
✚ C8 ✉ Desert Passage, 3663 Las Vegas Boulevard South ☎ 702/866-6624 🚋 Bally's/Paris 🖥 301, 302; Strip trolley

TRADER JOE'S

Founded in 1958 in LA, this old neighborhood grocery store prides itself on searching out one-of-a-kind products from around the world. Only the best is good enough for Trader Joe.
✚ Off map at A5 ✉ South Decatur Boulevard ☎ 702/367-0227 🖥 103

WINE CELLAR

An impressive selection of wines (more than 45,000 bottles) from the world's top viticulture regions is gathered here. Prices range from reasonable to astronomical for some of the rare vintages. Wine tastings are offered and experts are on hand to give advice.
✚ A7 ✉ Rio, 3700 West Flamingo Road ☎ 702/777-7962 🖥 202

Books & Music

ALBION BOOKS

You could spend hours browsing at this characterful secondhand bookstore, which includes obscure editions alongside classic titles.

➕ H6 ✉ 2466 East Desert Inn Road ☎ 702/792-9554 🚌 112

BARNES & NOBLE

This is one of several Vegas branches of the colossally well-stocked general bookstore. It has impressive children's and best-seller sections.

➕ F7 ✉ 3860 South Maryland Parkway ☎ 702/734-2900 🚌 109

BIG B'S CDS & RECORDS

Here is one of the best selections of old and new CDs and vinyl in town. As well as strong pop, rock, hip-hop and punk sections, the jazz, blues and country are also very good. Staff are helpful.

➕ F8 ✉ 4761 South Maryland Parkway ☎ 702/732-4433 🚌 109

BORDERS

At this international chain you can shop in a relaxed atmosphere. Browse the vast range of books, magazines, movies and music, then visit the in-store café. There are other branches in the city.

➕ Off map at A5 ✉ 2323 South Decatur Boulevard ☎ 702/258-0999 🚌 103

DEAD POET BOOKS

Among this jumble of antiquarian titles, you will find first editions, metaphysical cookbooks and military history.

➕ A5 ✉ 3874 West Sahara Avenue ☎ 702/227-4070 🚌 204

GAMBLER'S BOOK SHOP

This specialist bookstore has all the references you might need to prepare you for a flutter, whether it be at the tables or at the track. Don't be tempted by the video tutorials on cheating—casino staff are all too familiar with them. Game software is also sold here.

➕ F3 ✉ 630 South 11th Street ☎ 702/382-7555 🚌 109, 301, 302

GET BOOKED

Las Vegas' only gay and lesbian bookstore is a good source of information and sells books, magazines, cards, videos, posters and more.

➕ E8 ✉ 4640 Paradise Road ☎ 702/737-7780 🚌 108

SAM ASH

This megastore is a musicians' playground stacked high with guitars, amps, drums and brass and wind instruments of every conceivable brand.

➕ F5 ✉ 2747 Maryland Parkway ☎ 702/734-0007 🚌 109

TOWER RECORDS

A vast array of CDs, vinyl, videos, books and magazines is stocked at this huge superstore.

➕ Off map at A5 ✉ 4580 West Sahara Avenue ☎ 702/364-2500 🚌 204

BOOKSTORE CHAINS

If books are top of your shopping list in Las Vegas, you won't go home empty-handed. Nearly every mall has at least one bookstore, and you will find most major chains operating in or around the city somewhere. Look out for B. Dalton, Barnes & Noble, Book Warehouse, Borders and Walden.

Performance Showrooms/Venues

The most popular long-running shows and the new ones sell out quickly, so it's a good idea to make reservations. Call the relevant hotel or check out its website, which will have a reservation facility. Otherwise, shows can be reserved through TicketMaster (www.ticketmaster.com). Reservations are taken for long-running shows up to 30 days in advance; limited-time concerts or sporting events such as boxing matches can be reserved three months in advance.

ALADDIN CENTER FOR THE PERFORMING ARTS

Big-name stars perform here on a regular basis.
➕ C8 ✉ Aladdin, 3667 Las Vegas Boulevard South
☎ 702/785-5555
🚃 Bally's/Paris 🚌 301, 302; Strip trolley

COLOSSEUM

This Caesars Palace auditorium was purpose-built as the home of Céline Dion's *A New Day…* show (➤ 52).
➕ C7 ✉ Caesars Palace, 3570 Las Vegas Boulevard South
☎ 702/731-7333
🚃 Flamingo/Caesars 🚌 301, 302; Strip trolley

CONGO SHOWROOM

A lively schedule of musicians and comedians is on the bill here.
➕ D5 ✉ Sahara, 2535 Las Vegas Boulevard South
☎ 702/737-2111 🚃 Sahara 🚌 301, 302; Strip trolley

FLAMINGO SHOWROOM

The likes of Nat King Cole and Jerry Lewis have graced the stage here. Currently, soul singer Gladys Knight is appearing five nights a week, and so are top comedy group Second City.
➕ C7 ✉ Flamingo, 3555 Las Vegas Boulevard South
☎ 702/733-3333
🚃 Flamingo/Caesars 🚌 301, 302; Strip trolley

GRAND GARDEN ARENA

This is one of the biggest venues in town, hosting huge events ranging from top entertainers to world championship boxing.
➕ C8 ✉ MGM Grand, 3799 Las Vegas Boulevard South
☎ 702/891-7777 🚃 MGM Grand 🚌 301, 302; Strip trolley

HOLLYWOOD THEATER

MGM's smaller venue—hosting *La Femme*, an adaptation of the original show from the Crazy Horse in Paris, France—also puts on top-line comedy acts.
➕ C8 ✉ MGM Grand, 3799 Las Vegas Boulevard South
☎ 702/891-7777 🚃 MGM Grand 🚌 301, 302; Strip trolley

HOUSE OF BLUES

Bringing New Orleans to Las Vegas, this superb, 1,500-seat venue is on three levels and books such big-name stars as B. B. King and Brian Ferry. There's great food, including the popular Sunday Gospel Brunch. Check out the unusual artworks, too.
➕ C9 ✉ Mandalay Bay, 3950 Las Vegas Boulevard South
☎ 702/632-7600 🚌 301, 302; Strip trolley

THE JOINT

One of Vegas' hottest venues, with a capacity of 1,400, the Joint brings in cutting-edge bands that are worthy of the Hard Rock image.
➕ E8 ✉ Hard Rock, 4455 Paradise Road ☎ 702/693-5000 🚌 108

LAS VEGAS HILTON SHOWROOM

A variety of musicians, comedians and magicians perform here at reasonable prices.

⊞ E5 ✉ Las Vegas Hilton, 3000 Paradise Road ☎ 702/732-5755 🚇 Las Vegas Hilton 🚌 108

MANDALAY BAY EVENTS CENTER

This major boxing venue also hosts big-name concerts. On one night, usually in June, it is transformed into a gigantic nightclub for the "Summer of Love" event.

⊞ C9 ✉ Mandalay Bay, 3950 Las Vegas Boulevard South ☎ 0877/632-7580 🚌 301, 302; Strip trolley

ORLEANS ARENA

Since opening in 2004, this huge arena has hosted *Disney on Ice*, top concerts and a variety of sporting events.

⊞ A8 ✉ Orleans, 4500 West Tropicana ☎ 702/365-7469 🚌 201

LE THEATRE DES ARTS

Natalie Cole and Tony Bennet are among the artists who have performed at this 1,200-seat theater.

⊞ C7 ✉ Paris Las Vegas, 3645 Las Vegas Boulevard South ☎ 702/946-4567 🚇 Bally's/Paris 🚌 301, 302; Strip trolley

UNLV PERFORMING ARTS CENTER

Come here to enjoy major international artists performing classical and popular music, dance, theater, ballet and opera. The arts center comprises the Artemus W. Ham Concert Hall (home to the Nevada Symphony Orchestra), the Judy

Bayley Theatre and the Alta Ham Black Box Theatre.

⊞ F8 ✉ University of Nevada, 4505 South Maryland Parkway ☎ 702/895-2787 🚌 109

COMEDY

COMEDY CLUB

Four acts a night do stand-up at this comedy spot on the second floor of the Mardi Gras Plaza at the Riviera. Once a month the venue holds a light-night show for X-rated comedians.

⊞ D5 ✉ Riviera, 2901 Las Vegas Boulevard South ☎ 702/734-9301 🚌 301, 302; Strip trolley

COMEDY STOP

Every night of the week you can laugh at three top comedians here, any one of whom you would go a long way to see. Ray Romano, Tim Allen and Drew Carey are just a few of the well-known names who have performed at the venue.

⊞ C8 ✉ Tropicana, 3801 Las Vegas Boulevard South ☎ 702/739-2411 🚇 MGM Grand 🚌 301, 302; Strip trolley

THE IMPROV

Afternoon shows at this venue feature the incomparable Mac King, with his very unusual comedy magic. Later on in the day, emerging stars from a branch of the famous Improv comedy club take to the stage.

⊞ C7 ✉ Harrah's, 3475 Las Vegas Boulevard South ☎ 702/369-5111 🚇 Harrah's/Imperial Palace 🚌 301, 302; Strip trolley

THE BIG SCREEN

There are plenty of cinemas in Las Vegas where you can catch the latest blockbusters, and sparkling new multiplexes are popping up all over the place. For somewhere close to the Strip, try Century Orleans 18 (✉ Orleans, 4500 West Tropicana Avenue ☎ 702/227-3456), or if you are in the Downtown area, call in at Crown Theatres Neonopolis 14 (✉ 450 Fremont Street ☎ 702/383-9600). The city's only IMAX cinema is at the Luxor (✉ 3900 Las Vegas Boulevard South ☎ 702/262-4000).

Lounges & Bars

GAY BARS

Unlike most other aspects of Las Vegas, the city's gay scene is relatively discreet. Contact the Gay and Lesbian Center (✉ 812 East Sahara Avenue ☎ 702/733-9800) for information. The most popular bars and clubs include Gipsy (✉ 4605 East Paradise Road ☎ 702/731-1919), The Eagle (✉ 3430 East Tropicana Avenue ☎ 702/458-8862) and Good Times (✉ Liberace Plaza, 1775 East Tropicana Avenue ☎ 702/736-9494).

AVA

Relax in this exotic lounge amid jungle foliage and lulled by the soothing sound of waterfalls.
➕ C7 ✉ Mirage, 3400 Las Vegas Boulevard South ☎ 702/791-7111 🚍 301, 302; Strip trolley

BOURBON STREET CABARET

The New Orleans theme extends to the jazz trios that play here until the early hours.
➕ Off map at A8 ✉ Orleans, 4500 West Tropicana Avenue ☎ 702/365-7111 🚍 201

CASBAR LOUNGE

This is a real throwback to the Las Vegas of the 1970s, before any of today's sophistication set in. There's live entertainment nightly.
➕ D5 ✉ Sahara, 2535 Las Vegas Boulevard South ☎ 702/737-2111 🚇 Sahara 🚍 301, 302; Strip trolley

CELEBRATION LOUNGE AND HARBOR BAR

Entertaining singing bartenders here offer up anything from Frank Sinatra to Patsy Cline and still find time to serve some of the best margaritas in the city.
➕ C9 ✉ Tropicana, 3801 Las Vegas Boulevard South ☎ 702/739-2222 🚇 MGM Grand 🚍 301, 302; Strip trolley

COYOTE UGLY

If you enjoyed the movie or have visited the New York original, you'll love it here. It's a fun Southern-style saloon with wild bartenders who dance on the bar.
➕ C8 ✉ New York–New York, 3790 Las Vegas Boulevard South ☎ 702/212-8804 🚍 301, 301; Strip trolley

EIFFEL TOWER BAR

This sophisticated, elegant bar is located inside the restaurant, 11 floors up in the air. Stop by for a drink and at the same time take in the most stunning views of Las Vegas in all its glory.
➕ C7 ✉ Paris Las Vegas, 3655 Las Vegas Boulevard South ☎ 702/946-7000 🚇 Bally's/Paris 🚍 301, 302; Strip trolley

GHOST BAR

Apart from the fact that this sleek futuristic spot is *the* bar of the moment, you should also come for the fab views from the 55th floor of the Palms. Dress up and do battle with all the other beautiful people.
➕ A7 ✉ Palms Resort, 4321 West Flamingo Road ☎ 702/942-7778 🚍 202

GORDON-BIERSCH LAS VEGAS

Exposed pipes and gleaming brewing equipment set the stage for this hangout, popular with local yuppies. The beers include tasty German brews and are changed seasonally.
➕ E7 ✉ 3987 Paradise Road ☎ 702/312-5247 🚍 108

LUCKY'S LOOKOUT BALCONY

This is a great place to sit with a drink watching over the Fremont Street Experience below.
➕ F2 ✉ Fitzgeralds, 301 Fremont Street ☎ 702/388-2400 🚍 108, 301, 302

MIST BAR

A lively crowd comes to this relaxed spot, with its neighborhood-bar atmosphere, to watch sports on large plasma screens and to listen to rock and pop.
🔲 C6 ✉ Treasure Island, 3300 Las Vegas Boulevard South ☎ 702/894-7330 🚌 301, 302; Strip trolley

NAPOLEON'S

The French theme here incorporates French wines and beers, and French-style hot and cold appetizers. There are other imported beers, plus a cigar and pipe lounge and live entertainment.
🔲 C7 ✉ Paris Las Vegas, 3655 Las Vegas Boulevard South ☎ 702/946-6349 🚌 Bally's/Paris 🚌 301, 302; Strip trolley

OASIS LOUNGE

This classy Downtown lounge has a less pretentious ambience than many of its counterparts on the Strip. There is live music and other entertainment.
🔲 F2 ✉ Golden Nugget, 129 Fremont Street ☎ 702/385-7111 🚌 108, 301, 302

PEPPERMILL'S FIRESIDE LOUNGE

Shag carpeting, fire pits, enormous white silk flowers and indoor fountains are still the rage at this tribute to old-world Vegas.
🔲 D5 ✉ 2985 Las Vegas Boulevard South ☎ 702/735-7635 🚌 301, 302; Strip trolley

PETROSSIAN LOUNGE

Classy and romantic, the Petrossian lounge at the Bellagio is perfect for an intimate drink and laid-back live music.
🔲 C7 ✉ Bellagio, 3600 Las Vegas Boulevard South ☎ 702/693-7111 🚌 301, 302; Strip trolley

RED SQUARE

Red Square's Russian theme is visible in the headless statue of Lenin, the red-velvet drapes and the fake Communist propaganda. More than 100 Russian-inspired cocktails and fruit-infused vodkas are available, and the ice bar will keep your drink chilled. There's also a restaurant here (► 66).
🔲 C9 ✉ Mandalay Bay, 3950 Las Vegas Boulevard South ☎ 702/632-7407 🚌 301, 302; Strip trolley

TRIPLE 7 BREWPUB

The beers are the best reason to come to this modern Downtown microbrewery; there are five regulars on tap, including lagers, stouts and a good red. A simple menu and a sushi bar provide a light bite.
🔲 F2 ✉ Main Street Station, 200 North Main Street ☎ 702/387-1896 🚌 108, 301, 302

V BAR

Enclosed in opaque glass walls, this high-roller's joint oozes sophistication. Sleek lines, leather chaise longues and subdued lighting enhance the sultry atmosphere.
🔲 C7 ✉ Venetian, 3355 Las Vegas Boulevard South ☎ 702/414-1000 🚌 301, 302; Strip trolley

WHAT'S THE DIFFERENCE?

Bars are usually more lively than lounges but have a cover charge. They often serve light meals and offer more of a "scene." Lounges, on the other hand, are free of a cover charge, and they have more pleasant seating and better drinks than you'll find on the casino floor. Both bars and lounges provide live entertainment.

Nightclubs

DRESS CODES AND DOOR POLICIES

Most, if not all, of the nightclubs listed here impose quite a strict dress code, so it's a good idea to check what is acceptable beforehand. Men will have more trouble than women when it comes to what they are wearing: Jeans and sneakers are guaranteed to keep hopefuls out of any club. Women are also more likely to get in when there are long lines. You can get onto the VIP list if you know someone who works at the club, or if you have spent a lot in the casino. Otherwise, join the line outside the door (about an hour before opening time at the most popular places) and hope for the best. Cover charges, where they exist, are usually less than $20, and may be at different rates for men and women.

THE BEACH

This loud, tropical-themed hot spot over two levels is built around a huge dance floor that is always crammed with fun-seekers. Bikini-clad girls and guys in surf shorts serve free shots of tequila. Each night sees something different.
➕ E6 ✉ 365 Convention Center Drive ☎ 702/731-1925 🚌 108, 301, 302; Strip trolley

BODY ENGLISH

Cave-like booths and innovative design create elegance with an edge at this buzzing two-tiered, dance club. The energetic music avoids the endless techno drone.
➕ E8 ✉ Hard Rock Hotel, 4455 Paradise Road ☎ 702/693-5000 🚌 108

CLEOPATRA'S BARGE

The name reveals the theme at this floating club. During the week, a DJ plays contemporary dance music, and there's live music on weekends.
➕ C7 ✉ Caesars Palace, 3570 Las Vegas Boulevard South ☎ 702/731-7110 🚌 301, 302; Strip trolley

CLUB RIO

This is one of the originals of the city's club scene (it was the first to introduce Latin music), and has state-of-the-art sound-and-light systems.
➕ A7 ✉ Rio, 3700 West Flamingo Road ☎ 702/252-7777 🚌 202

ICE

Six different-themed party rooms here offer music and cocktails, while three dance floors pump out techno, hip-hop, house and funk. An outdoor courtyard hosts live bands.
➕ D8 ✉ 200 East Harmon Avenue ☎ 702/699-9888 🚌 213

THE NIGHTCLUB

This classy, art deco-style club steps up with a live band rather than DJs after the headliners have finished.
➕ E5 ✉ Las Vegas Hilton, 3000 Paradise Road ☎ 702/732-5111 🚇 Las Vegas Hilton 🚌 108

RA

House music, top DJs and go-go dancers set the scene at this chic Egyptian-themed club. On Wednesdays is the "X-treme house party."
➕ C9 ✉ Luxor, 3900 Las Vegas Boulevard South ☎ 702/262-4000 🚌 301, 302; Strip trolley

RUMJUNGLE

This hot club has a Caribbean theme and some breathtaking features—acrobats in harnesses "fly" across the ceiling and there is a wall of flames and a waterfall.
➕ C9 ✉ Mandalay Bay, 3950 Las Vegas Boulevard South ☎ 702/632-7408 🚌 301, 302; Strip trolley

STUDIO 54

Celebrities come to this high-energy club, an exact replica of the famous 1970s original in New York.
➕ C8 ✉ MGM Grand, 3799 Las Vegas Boulevard South ☎ 702/891-7777 🚇 MGM Grand 🚌 301, 302; Strip trolley

Sports & Activities

GOLF

ANGEL PARK GOLF CLUB
Experience both mountains and palms at this 36-hole course designed by legendary golfer Arnold Palmer. Views over Red Rock Canyon and the valley are spectacular.
🔼 Off map at A2 ✉ 100 South Rampart Boulevard, 3 miles (5km) west of US95 at Summerlin Parkway ☎ 702/254-0566

BALI HAI GOLF CLUB
A South Pacific theme pervades this course, with outcrops of volcanic rock, groups of palm trees and white sand in the bunkers.
🔼 C10 ✉ 5160 Las Vegas Boulevard ☎ 702/405-8000; www.waltergolf.com 🚌 301, 302; Strip trolley

LAS VEGAS NATIONAL GOLF CLUB
Opened in 1961, this classic 18-hole course has glistening lakes. In 1996, champion golfer Tiger Woods won his first PGA victory here.
🔼 H6 ✉ 1911 Desert Inn Road ☎ 702/734-1796 🚌 112

ROYAL LINKS GOLF CLUB
This golf club has holes patterned after the most famous ones on courses used in the British Open. In keeping with the British theme, the 18th hole resembles a medieval castle.
🔼 Off map at H6 ✉ 5995 East Vegas Valley Road, 6 miles (10km) east of Las Vegas Boulevard ☎ 702/450-8000

TENNIS

There are many places in Vegas to play tennis. UNLV (☎ 702/895-0844) has 12 courts for general use, and Desert Palm Tennis Club (✉ 3090 South Jones Boulevard ☎ 702/368-2800) offers excellent facilities. Most hotel courts are open to nonguests, although guests take priority; try Flamingo, Monte Carlo or Bally's. You can play for free at Sunset Park (✉ 2601 East Sunset), which has eight courts.

OTHER ACTIVITIES

A. J. HACKETT BUNGEE
The Las Vegas facility of this worldwide company has North America's highest double platform jump (171ft/52m).
🔼 D5 ✉ 810 Circus Circus Drive ☎ 702/385-4321; www.aj-hackett.com 🚌 301, 302; Strip trolley

COWBOY TRAIL RIDES
Guided horseback tours can be arranged through Red Rock Canyon (► 50) and Mount Charleston (► 62). They include transportation to and from your hotel. Reserve ahead.
☎ 702/387-2457; www.cowboytrailrides.com

ORLEANS BOWLING CENTER
Tournaments are held at this 70-lane bowling alley, so check before making an evening visit.
🔼 A8 ✉ Orleans, 4500 West Tropicana Avenue ☎ 702/365-7111 🚌 201

MAJOR EVENTS
Las Vegas has become the home of some of the world's most impressive sporting events. World title heavyweight boxing bouts are fought in the city's arenas, and WWF and WCW wrestlers take part in major events in the city as well. Las Vegas is also the site of the Las Vegas Motor Speedway, which has become one of the top raceways in the world, attracting such major competitions as the Winston Cup and other major races.

Luxury Hotels

PRICES

Average prices for a double room per night:

Luxury = more than $250
Mid-range = $100–$250
Budget = less than $100

HOTEL GRADING

US hotels, including those in Las Vegas, are classified by the American Automobile Association (AAA, or Triple A) into five categories, from one to five diamonds. As this is based entirely on facilities offered, it does mean that hotels with four diamonds can be equally as luxurious as those with five, or that an attractively furnished atmospheric two-diamond bed-and-breakfast may cost less than a down-at-heel three-diamond business hotel.

BELLAGIO (➤ 34)

Set behind an enormous lake, this is one of the most beautiful hotels in Vegas, built in the style of a huge Mediterranean villa with lovely gardens. The 3,000-plus rooms and suites are large and classy, decorated in natural hues.

➕ C7 ✉ 3600 Las Vegas Boulevard South ☎ 702/693-7111; fax 702/693-8546; www.bellagio.com 🚌 301, 302; Strip trolley

CAESARS PALACE (➤ 35)

Caesars' theme is ancient Rome, with classical temples, marble columns and every possible excess you can imagine. All 2,419 rooms and suites are luxurious, but even more so in the tower, where there are huge whirlpool tubs in the bathrooms.

➕ C7 ✉ 3570 Las Vegas Boulevard South ☎ 702/731-7110; fax 702/731-6636; www.caesars.com/palace 🚌 301, 302; Strip trolley

FOUR SEASONS

This hotel takes up the top five levels of the Mandalay Bay (➤ this page), but retains its own tranquil identity. The 424 rooms and suites are elegantly decorated in peach, aqua and gold, and while it provides a peaceful haven, all the Mandalay Bay facilities are available to guests.

➕ C9 ✉ 3960 Las Vegas Boulevard South ☎ 702/632-5000; fax 702/632-5195; www.fourseasons.com 🚌 301, 302; Strip trolley

MANDALAY BAY

There is masses of big-city style here, with 2 nightclubs and 13 restaurants. It's the only hotel in Las Vegas with a beach and a gigantic wave pool. There are 3,000-plus rooms and suites; even the standard rooms are huge, and all are light and airy.

➕ C9 ✉ 3950 Las Vegas Boulevard South ☎ 702/632-7777; fax 702/632-7190; www.mandalaybay.com 🚌 301, 302; Strip trolley

THE VENETIAN (➤ 38)

Famous for its canals and replica of St. Mark's Square, the Venetian has 4,049 rooms (actually they are all suites). The decor varies, although all have marble bathrooms and fine funishings.

➕ C7 ✉ 3855 Las Vegas Boulevard South ☎ 702/414-1000; fax 702/414-4805; www.venetian.com 🚌 301, 302; Strip trolley

WYNN LAS VEGAS

The doors opened on Steve Wynn's latest incredible hotel-casino in April 2005. It is the world's most expensive hotel and has 50 floors with 2,716 rooms and suites. There's a private lake, a man-made mountain and an 18-hole golf course. The very stylish rooms and suites are huge, and are equipped with every concievable luxury.

➕ D6 ✉ 3131 Las Vegas Boulevard South ☎ 702/770-7100; fax 702/770-1571; www.wynnlasvegas.com 🚇 Las Vegas Convention Center 🚌 301, 302; Strip trolley

Mid-Range Hotels

ALEXIS PARK

If you prefer to stay off the Strip, this small hotel, with just 496 rooms, has some great two-level suites for a really good price. It's also fairly quiet here. Facilities include a spa.
✚ E8 ✉ 375 East Harmon Avenue ☎ 702/796-3300; fax 702/796-4334; www.alexispark.com 🛏 213

BALLY'S LAS VEGAS

More sedate than many Vegas hotels, Bally's is less oriented toward a lively young crowd or families. The 2,814 rooms and suites are particularly sumptuous, with grand sitting rooms and opulent bathrooms. Facilities include floodlit tennis courts.
✚ C7 ✉ 3645 Las Vegas Boulevard South ☎ 702/739-4111; fax 702/967-4405; www.ballyslv.com 🚇 Bally's/Paris 🛏 301, 302; Strip trolley

FLAMINGO LAS VEGAS

Bugsy Siegel's original 1946 Flamingo was rebuilt by the Hilton group in 1993. The modern hotel has 3,565 units in all; the deluxe king rooms are very spacious. The Flamingo also has one of the best pool areas on the Strip.
✚ C7 ✉ 3555 Las Vegas Boulevard South ☎ 702/733-3111; fax 702/733-3355; www.lv-flamingo.com 🚇 Flamingo/Caesars 🛏 301, 302; Strip trolley

LUXOR

This 4,407-room, pyramid-shaped hotel is Egyptian-themed right down to its foundations. You enter beneath a huge sphinx and are taken to your room via an elevator that travels up the pyramid's slope.
✚ C9 ✉ 3900 Las Vegas Boulevard South ☎ 702/262-4000; fax 702/262-4454; www.luxor.com 🛏 108

MGM GRAND

The MGM Grand is pure Hollywood, with figures of stars dotted around the lobby and huge stills from movies on the walls. The 5,000-plus rooms offer a range of options, from the small Emerald Tower rooms to spacious suites.
✚ C8 ✉ 3799 Las Vegas Boulevard South ☎ 702/891-1111; fax 702/891-1030; www.mgmgrand.com 🚇 MGM Grand 🛏 301, 302; Strip trolley

MONTE CARLO

A popular choice with golfers (it has a full-time golf concierge), the Monte Carlo has 3,000 or so attractive rooms and suites; those at the front have good views.
✚ C8 ✉ 3770 Las Vegas Boulevard South ☎ 702/730-7777; fax 702/730-7250; www.monte-carlo.com 🛏 301, 302; Strip trolley

RIO ALL-SUITE HOTEL AND CASINO

This is a lively hotel in an off-Strip location, with great nightlife and two excellent buffets among its dining options. It has 2,548 huge rooms and suites.
✚ A7 ✉ 3700 Flamingo Road ☎ 702/777-7777; fax 702/777-2294; www.playrio.com 🛏 202

THE HOTEL EXPERIENCE

The fanciful hotel architecture of Las Vegas means that many people come here for the hotel experience alone. Some rarely leave the premises—quite understandable when there's an on-site casino, a choice of superb restaurants, world-class shows and shopping, luxury spas and plenty of other leisure amenities. On the downside, the large hotels can suffer from slow service and long lines for checking in and out, though express check-out boxes are available in many cases. You simply drop off your keys and leave, and your credit card is charged about a week later. If you are going to stay in a very large hotel, try to get a room near the elevator.

Budget Hotels

BEST OF BOTH WORLDS

With so much to do and see in Las Vegas, you probably won't be spending much time in your hotel room. In view of this—and the fact that most hotel rooms look pretty much the same—it might not make sense to pay out for an expensive room just for sleeping and storing your luggage. It is perfectly possible to stay in a lower price hotel, but spend your waking hours in the fancier establishments.

CIRCUS CIRCUS (► 42)

Although it is one of the oldest hotels on the Strip, after recent refurbishments Circus Circus still provides one of the best value-for-money options if you have kids with you. It has 3,744 rooms.
➕ D5 ✉ 2880 Las Vegas Boulevard South ☎ 702/734-0410; fax 702/734-5897; www.circuscircus.com 🚌 301, 302; Strip trolley

COURTYARD BY MARRIOT

Part of the well-known chain, this hotel provides 149 nicer-than-the-average motel rooms.
➕ E7 ✉ 3275 Paradise Road ☎ 702/791-3600; fax 702/796-7981; www.courtyard.com 🚌 108

EXCALIBUR (► 28)

Kids love this medieval castle, with its moat and drawbridge. Parents might find it all just a little tacky, but it's probably the best deal on the Strip, and has 3,991 comfortable, peaceful rooms.
➕ C9 ✉ 3850 Las Vegas Boulevard South ☎ 702/597-7777; fax 702/597-7009; www.excalibur.com 🚌 301, 302; Strip trolley

HOWARD JOHNSON SHALIMAR

The Shalimar is a low-rise motel in a good location on the Strip. Some of the 104 rooms have a whirlpool bath.
➕ E4 ✉ 1401 Las Vegas Boulevard South ☎ 702/388-0301; fax 702/388-2506; www.vegasinns.com 🚌 301, 302; Strip trolley

MAIN STREET STATION

This lovely hotel has a Victorian theme, with genuine antiques, flickering gas lamps, iron railings and stained-glass windows. The 452 bright rooms offer a great bargain.
➕ F2 ✉ 200 North Main Street ☎ 702/387-1896; fax 702/386-4466; www.mainstreetcasino.com 🚌 108

SOMERSET HOUSE MOTEL

Handy for the Convention Center, and just one block off the Strip, this good-value motel has 104 rooms and minisuites.
➕ D6 ✉ 294 Convention Center Drive ☎ 702/735-4411; fax 702/369-2388; www.somerset-house.com 🚇 Las Vegas Convention Center 🚌 108, 301, 302; Strip trolley

STARDUST

This likeable hotel, opened in 1958, is part of Las Vegas' history and has retained its old gambling image. The 1,550 rooms are newly remodeled.
➕ D6 ✉ 3000 Las Vegas Boulevard South ☎ 702/732-6111; fax 702/732-6257; www.stardustlv.com 🚌 108

TERRIBLE'S

Don't be fooled by the name, as this small hotel very near the Strip is anything but terrible. The 374 pleasant rooms are basic but clean, at very agreeable rates.
➕ E7 ✉ 4100 Paradise Road ☎ 702/733-7000; fax 702/765-5109; www.terribleherbst.com 🚌 108

LAS VEGAS
travel facts

ESSENTIAL FACTS

Customs regulations

- Visitors from outside the US, age 21 or over, may import duty-free: 200 cigarettes, or 50 non-Cuban cigars, or 2kg of tobacco; 1 liter of alcohol; and gifts up to $100 in value.
- The import of wildlife souvenirs sourced from rare or endangered species may either be illegal or require a special permit. Before purchase you should check your home country's customs regulations.
- Restricted import items include meat, seeds, plants and fruit.
- Some medication bought over the counter abroad may be prescription-only in the US and could be confiscated. Bring a doctor's certificate for essential medication.

Electricity

- Voltage is 110/120 volts AC (60 cycles) and sockets take two-prong, flat-pin plugs. European appliances also need a voltage transformer.

Etiquette

- Tip staff at least 15–20 percent in a restaurant, taxi drivers $1–$2 for a direct route, porters $1–$2 per bag depending on the distance carried, and valet parking attendants $1–$2.
- Las Vegas is one of the few pro-smoking places left in the US. Most restaurants have designated smoking areas.
- Dress is very informal during the day, and shorts and T-shirts are generally accepted anywhere. In the evening smart-casual is more the norm, and some lounges, nightclubs and restaurants may have a dress code.

Lavatories

- Clean, free public restrooms are found throughout the city in hotels, casinos, restaurants and bars.

Money and credit cards

- Credit cards are widely accepted.
- Most banks have ATMs.
- US-dollar travelers' checks are accepted as cash in most places, but ID may be requested.
- Most major hotels will exchange foreign currency, and there are several exchange bureaus on the Strip. You can also change money at major banks, most of which are located off the Strip.

National holidays

- Jan 1: New Year's Day
- 3rd Mon in Jan: Martin Luther King Jr. Day
- 3rd Mon in Feb: President's Day
- Mar/Apr: Easter (half-day holiday on Good Friday)
- Last Mon in May: Memorial Day
- Jul 4: Independence Day
- 1st Mon in Sep: Labor Day
- 2nd Mon in Oct: Columbus Day
- Nov 11: Veterans' Day
- 4th Thu in Nov: Thanksgiving
- Dec 25: Christmas Day

Opening hours

- Banks: generally Mon–Fri 9–3 or later, and some Sat mornings.
- Post offices: normally Mon–Fri 8.30–6, with limited hours on Sat.
- Stores: usually open at 10am; closing times vary, and may be later on weekends.
- Museums: see individual entries for details.
- Las Vegas boasts that it never closes and never sleeps, but off-Strip stores and banks, and peripheral businesses, will be closed on certain holidays.

Student travelers

• Discounts are sometimes available to students who have an International Student Identification Card (ISIC).

Tourist information office

• Las Vegas Visitor Information Center: ✉ 3150 Paradise Road, Las Vegas, NV 89109 ☎ 702/892-0711; fax 702/892-2824; www.vegasfreedom.

Visitors with disabilities (► 7)

• Vegas has several elevated crosswalks to and from the main hotels that are accessible by elevator, making sidewalk travel in a wheelchair easier.

• All hotels are accessible to visitors with disabilities. If you have any special needs, talk to the hotel concierge, who will always be happy to help. Hotel pools often have lifts to assist entry and exit.

• All shows offer seating for visitors with disabilities. Many venues have assisted listening devices for audience members with hearing impairments.

• Many attractions and rides are accessible, although there are limitations on some; check ahead.

GETTING AROUND (► 7)

Buses and trams

• CAT (Citizens Area Transit ☎ 702/228-7433) buses run every 10 minutes, 24 hours a day, from the Downtown Transportation Center at Stewart Avenue and Casino Center Boulevard down the Strip, with stops along the way. The fare is $2 one-way (you need to have the exact fare because drivers can't give change) and you can get a transfer from the driver for off-Strip destinations, so you don't have to pay again. Off-strip buses otherwise cost $1.25 one-way. Hotels should have timetables for the citywide system; if not, call the number above.

Car rental

• Hotel information desks can advise about renting a car. Rental companies deliver to your hotel and pick up again at the end of the rental period.

Driving

• Almost every hotel on Las Vegas Boulevard South has its own self-parking garage. The best way into them, avoiding the gridlock on the Strip, is via the back entrances. Valet parking is also available at the front (and sometimes other) entrances. The standard tip for valets is $1, or $2 if they are particularly speedy.

• The best advice about driving in Las Vegas is don't do it unless you really have to.

• The speed limit on the Strip is 35mph (56kph). The wearing of seat belts is compulsory.

Monorails

• The eagerly awaited state-of-the-art monorail (see box ► 12) opened in 2004. Running from MGM Grand to the Sahara, it operates every day from 7pm to 2am. There are seven stations: MGM Grand, Bally's/Paris, Flamingo/Caesars, Harrah's/Imperial Palace, Las Vegas Convention Center, Las Vegas Hilton and Sahara. A single fare costs $3, a 10-ride ticket is $20, a one-day pass is $10 and a three-day pass costs $25.

• There are also a number of smaller free monorail services

courtesy of the hotels, including one between the Mandalay Bay, the Excalibur and the Luxor (4am–2am), and one between the Bellagio and Monte Carlo (24 hours).

Taxis and limousines
- Taxis line up outside every hotel and you can call for one from your room. If you are already out, you need to call or go to a cab stand; taxis can't be hailed in the street.
- Taxi drivers are a good source of information. They have firsthand experience of all the shows and attractions, and can offer a review and make recommendations. For this service you should give more of a tip than the standard $1 or $2 for a straightforward journey. Also give a bigger tip if they help with the door and your luggage.
- There are plenty of limousine services, which start at $35 per hour (2 hour minimum). Your hotel concierge can make the necessary arrangements.

Trolleys
- The red-and-green trolley (☎ 702/382-1404) plies the Strip from 9.30am to 2am, stopping at each hotel along the boulevard every 15 minutes. You need to have the exact fare of $1.65.

Walking
- The Strip is 3.5 miles (5.5km) long, and it's a taxing walk in the heat of the day. Wear comfortable shoes and sunglasses.
- Even if you use the Strip's bus services, you will still have to walk considerable distances to and from the hotels, casinos and attractions.
- Overhead walkways connect several properties along the Strip.

- Making a note of the cross streets that punctuate the Strip will help you to find your bearings. Some are named after the hotels along them, which also aids navigation.

MEDIA & COMMUNICATIONS

Newspapers and magazines
- Las Vegas has two daily newspapers: the *Las Vegas Review Journal* and the *Las Vegas Sun*.
- Weeklies with club listings and restaurant and bar reviews include *City Life* and *Las Vegas Weekly*.

Post offices
- Main post office: ✉ 1001 East Sunset Road, between Paradise Road and Maryland Parkway ☎ 800/275-8777 🕐 Mon–Fri 7.30–9, Sat 8–4.
- There are many post offices in the city. You can also mail letters and parcels from your hotel.
- You can buy stamps from shops and from machines.
- US mailboxes are red and white.

Telephones
- There are public payphones in hotels, casinos, stores, restaurants, gas stations and on many street corners. You will need a good supply of quarters (overseas calls cost at least $5.50). Local calls from a phone booth cost around 35 cents. Some phones are equipped to take prepaid phone cards and/or charge cards and credit cards. Dial 1 plus the area code for numbers within the United States and Canada.
- Calls made from hotel rooms are very expensive.
- Information ☎ 411.
- Las Vegas' area code is 702, which does not need to be dialed if you are calling within the city.

- To call Las Vegas from the UK, dial 00 followed by 1 (the code for the US and Canada), then the number. To call the UK from Las Vegas, dial 00 44, then drop the first zero from the area code.

EMERGENCIES

Emergency telephone numbers
- Police ☎ 911.
- Fire ☎ 911.
- Ambulance ☎ 911.
- American Automobile Association (AAA) breakdown service ☎ 800/222-4357.

Lost property
- For property lost on public transportation: ✉ 6675 South Strip Transfer Terminal, South Gillespie Street ☎ 702/228-7433 🕐 Mon–Fri 7–5.30.
- For property lost at McCarran International Airport: ☎ 702/261-5134 🕐 Daily 6.30am–1am.
- Report losses of passports or credit cards to the police.

Medicines and medical treatment
- In medical emergencies ☎ 911 or go to the casualty department of the nearest hospital. Emergency-room services are available 24 hours at University Medical Center ✉ 1800 West Charleston Boulevard ☎ 702/383-2000, or Sunrise Hospital and Medical Center ✉ 3186 Maryland Parkway ☎ 702/731-8080.
- Pharmacies are indicated by a large green or red cross.
- Pharmacy telephone numbers are listed under "Pharmacies" or "Drugstores" in the Yellow Pages. Many will deliver medication to your hotel.

- 24-hour and night pharmacies are available at Walgreens ✉ 3763 Las Vegas Boulevard ☎ 702/739-9638, and at Sav-On ✉ 1360 East Flamingo Road at Maryland Parkway ☎ 702/731-5373.

Sensible precautions
- Carry only as much money with you as you need; leave other cash and valuables in the hotel safe.
- At night, especially if you are a woman alone, avoid hotel parking lots and always enter the hotel via the main entrance. If renting an apartment, use valet parking.
- Report theft or mugging on the street to the police department immediately.
- Make sure your room is locked when you leave. Some hotels change your locks and keys on a daily basis for security reasons.

GLOSSARY OF CASINO TERMS

Action Gaming activity measured by the amount wagered.
Bank The person covering the bets in any game, usually the casino.
Buy in Purchasing of chips.
Cage The cashier's section of the casino.
Even money A bet that pays off at one to one.
House edge The mathematical advantage the casino enjoys on every game and wager.
House odds The ratio at which the casino pays off a winning bet.
Limit The minimum/maximum bet accepted at a gambling table.
Loose machine A slot machine that is set to return a high percentage of the money played in.
Marker An IOU owed to the casino by someone playing on credit.
Toke A tip or gratuity.

93

Index

CityPack
Las Vegas *Top 25*

ABOUT THE AUTHORS
Expert travel writers Jackie Staddon, Hilary Weston and Penny Phenix all live in the south of England and specialise in writing and contributing to travel publications. Their love of travel has taken them to many parts of the world, and they all agree that Las Vegas has a particular appeal.

WRITTEN BY Jackie Staddon and Hilary Weston
ADDITIONAL WRITING Penny Phenix
MANAGING EDITOR Allen Stidwill

A CIP catalogue record for this book is available from the British Library.

ISBN 0-7495-4747-2
ISBN 978-0-7495-4747-9

Published by AA Publishing, a trading name of Automobile Association Developments Limited, whose registered office is Fanum House, Basing View, Basingstoke, Hampshire RG21 4EA. Registered number 1878835.

© **AUTOMOBILE ASSOCIATION DEVELOPMENTS LIMITED 2006**
First published 2006
Colour separation by Keenes
Printed and bound by Hang Tai D&P Limited, Hong Kong.

ACKNOWLEDGMENTS
The Automobile Association wishes to thank the following photographers, libraries and associations for their assistance in the preparation of this book.
© 2003 BELLAGIO GALLERY OF FINE ART (PHOTOGRAPH BY GREG HOFFMAN) 56CL; CAESARS ENTERTAINMENT, INC 54; GETTY IMAGES 16r; GETTY IMAGES/TIME LIFE PICTURES 16l, 17l; GUGGENHEIM HERMITAGE MUSEUM 39; IMPERIAL PALACE AUTO COLLECTIONS 36t, 36b; LAS VEGAS CONVENTION & VISITORS AUTHORITY 1t, 1, 2, 4, 6t, 8l, 8r, 9t, 9cr, 10t, 10, 11, 12t, 12/3, 13t, 13, 14t, 14, 15l, 15r, 16t, 17r, 18t, 18l, 18/9, 19t, 19c, 19r, 20tl, 22tl, 24t, 24r, 26, 31, 32b, 41br, 50, 51tr, 55, 59, 61, 62, 63t, 63b, 89t, 89bl; LAS VEGAS NATURAL HISTORY MUSEUM 47t, 47b; LIBERACE MUSEUM 29t, 29br; LIED DISCOVERY CHILDREN'S MUSEUM 56bl; COURTESY OF THE NEON MUSEUM, LAS VEGAS, NV 57; SAHARA HOTEL AND CASINO 43t, 43b; STAR TREK EXPERIENCE 25, 41t; STOCKBYTE 5.
All remaining images are held in the Associations own library (AA WORLD TRAVEL LIBRARY) with contributions from the following photographers:
L DUNMIRE 7, 8b, 8/9, 9br, 12, 15t, 21cr, 21br, 22tr, 22ctl, 22cbl, 22bl, 23tl, 23cr, 23br, 24l, 27, 30, 32t, 33, 34, 35, 37, 38, 40, 42, 44, 46, 51br, 58, 60; M VAN VARK 20tr, 20c, 28, 45, 48, 49; J WYAND 8c, 11t.

A02378
Cover maps produced from map data supplied by Global Mapping, Brackley, UK. Copyright © Global Mapping
Sheet map supplied by Global Mapping, Brackley, UK. Copyright © Global Mapping
Transport map © Communicarta Ltd, UK

TITLES IN THE CITYPACK SERIES
• Amsterdam • Bangkok • Barcelona • Beijing • Berlin • Boston • Brussels & Bruges • Chicago • Dublin • • Edinburgh • Florence • Hong Kong • Istanbul • Las Vegas • Lisbon • London • Los Angeles • Madrid • • Melbourne • Miami • Milan • Montréal • Munich • Naples • New York • Orlando • Paris • Prague • • Rome • San Francisco • Seattle • Shanghai • Singapore • Sydney • Tokyo • Toronto • Venice • Vienna • • Washington DC •